FINANCIAL
FITNESS

FINANCIAL
FITNESS

THE OFFENSE, DEFENSE, AND PLAYING FIELD OF PERSONAL FINANCE

NEW YORK TIMES BESTSELLING AUTHORS

CHRIS BRADY
ORRIN WOODWARD

OBSTACLÉS
PRESS

Published by:

Obstaclés Press
200 Commonwealth Court
Cary, NC 27511

Scripture quotations marked "KJV" are taken from The Holy Bible, King James Version, Cambridge, 1769.

Scripture quotations marked "NKJV" are taken from The New King James Version/Thomas Nelson Publishers, Nashville: Thomas Nelson Publishers, copyright © 1982. Used by permission. All rights reserved.

financialfitnessinfo.com

ISBN: 978-0-9858020-5-9

Second Edition, May 2015
10 9 8 7

Book design by Norm Williams, nwa-inc.com

Printed in the United States of America

This book is dedicated to all those who choose deliberate excellence over complacent mediocrity.

CONTENTS

PROLOGUE

Citizens of the world are drowning in debt. Between student loans, car loans, credit card balances, and home mortgages, people are having an increasingly difficult time keeping their heads above water. Even a cursory look at the latest American debt numbers (the data from around the civilized world is equally alarming) is enough to sober the most optimistic among us. According to GoBankingRates, an organization which tracks interest and banking rates, the average American is more than $225,000 in debt with many having less than $500 in savings!

Here is a summary of the American statistics broken out per category of debt:

- Average credit card debt among indebted households: $15,263
- Average credit card interest rate: 14.95% APR
- Average mortgage debt: $147,591
- Average outstanding student loan balance: $31,646
- Average auto loan debt: $30,738
- Percentage of Americans with at least $500 in a savings account: 59%

Unfortunately, the bad news doesn't end there. According to the latest U.S. Census Bureau data, the real (inflation adjusted) median household income was $51,939 in 2013. This income, one must not forget, is the combined incomes for everyone working in the household, which indicates the average salary is not much higher than $30,000 per year. Moreover, household income has been trending downward (a drop of nearly 8%) since its 1999 peak of $56,895.

In other words, for the last sixteen years, household income has gone down, while inflation has caused the prices of practically everything else to skyrocket. Remember $1 gas or $1 bread? Imagine working for less money every year for sixteen consecutive years while inflation more than doubles the cost of living. That is the beginning of understanding the modern debt dilemma. Simply put, price increases with pay decreases have caused an explosion of debt, which can only lead to an implosion of the world economy if not addressed immediately.

Modern civilization, in sum, exerts a hidden control over its citizens through the financial system. That system is the Financial Matrix. Interestingly, however, the people are not coerced into the Financial Matrix; rather, they are enticed into it. Companies and banks, through offering monthly payments on big-ticket items, seduce people into financial bondage. This book teaches the truth about the economic playing field (Financial Matrix) and offers a step-by-step financial plan for defense and offense to escape the debt system.

Our discovery of the Financial Matrix is eerily similar to Neo's discovery of the Matrix in the movie entitled *The Matrix*. In several scenes, Morpheus reveals to Neo that the world is not as it seems and that a Matrix controls the masses whether they are working, playing, or sleeping. The Matrix is "the world that has been pulled over your eyes, to blind you from the truth." Neo asks what truth Morpheus is referring to and learns, "That you are a slave, Neo. Like everyone else, you were born into bondage, born into a prison that you cannot smell or taste or touch. A prison for your mind....Unfortunately, no one can be told what the Matrix is. You have to see it for yourself."[1]

Morpheus places two pills before Neo and explains
that if he takes the blue pill, he will live an illusion
and never escape the Matrix, but if he takes the red
pill, he will learn the truth about the Matrix and how
to set himself free. In a similar fashion, the Financial
Fitness Program was designed to speak truth to
people caught in the Financial Matrix. If you, like
Neo, have been searching for answers, the good news
is that the search is over. The blue and red pills have
been placed before you. Your destiny awaits your next
move. Choose wisely.

Introduction

Think back to your earliest memories about money. When did you first realize that money had the power to purchase the things you wanted? When did you first wish you had enough money for something? When was the first time you were told you couldn't have something because you couldn't afford it? When was the first time you remember holding a lot of money in your hand and feeling really happy about it?

Now ask yourself another question: When you think back on your earliest memories about money, do the memories make you feel mostly positive or negative? For many people, early memories about money are often associated with a sense of lacking, of not having enough for something they wanted. Sadly, this feeling of lack, which we call "the money thing," is too often the way many people still feel today.

This feeling comes with the realization that you can't afford something you really desire, or that you don't have the resources to do something you really want to do, or even that you aren't able to help someone you care about simply because you lack the necessary money. Most importantly, "the money thing" sometimes keeps people from fully achieving their potential and living their deepest purposes in life.

Of course, there are a number of things that are more important than money, but "the money thing" is a limiting factor for far too many people. Both of us experienced this challenge during our youth, and as adults, we set out to discover how to overcome it. Here are our stories:

Chris's Story

As far back as I can remember I wanted to succeed financially. I guess I learned early that money was a necessary tool, and if lacking, was instead a major inhibitor. I wouldn't say I ever went as far as greedy materialism; rather, I was focused more on "making it" and eliminating "the money thing." It seemed as if money was a roadblock in many people's lives, obstructing their paths and telling them they could proceed no further.

"We can't afford it" was a phrase I grew up hearing a lot, both at home and from many people in my community. It seemed to be the major limit for most people.

But as a young person, I wondered, "Why can't I grow up and make a bunch of money? Why can't I find a way to kill the money limiter once and for all and be free to live my life the way I desire, rather than being hindered by a lack of money at every turn?"

So, of course, I began chasing financial success through the fantasy of becoming a professional motocross racer. It was only a teenage fantasy and quickly dissipated in the face of several facts—the first being that I wasn't good enough! So I shifted gears, so to speak, and embraced the "go to school, get good grades, get a good job, and work your way up the corporate ladder" philosophy of success. This produced some results and a decent income, but it was also like wearing someone else's shoes—fine for someone else but not fitting for me. I was working as an engineer at General Motors at the time, but something just didn't feel quite right.

A crossroads in my life came one day when I found myself on a Caribbean beach asking some very important questions: "Is this it? Is this all there is? Is this the life I want? Should I settle for good, or should I risk it all and go after my dreams?"

This experience helped me step off the "normal" path of a good job and a life in the suburbs to truly living my dreams. But the path wasn't easy. After I became an entrepreneur and went through many starts and stops, I finally found my way to the types of income I had always desired. This, however, was not enough. Making money was only the "offense" of personal finances. I still had many lessons to learn about the "defensive" side of finances and the preservation and proper stewardship of wealth.

It was through careless handling, hopeful and naïve investing, and many hard knocks, losses, bad decisions, unscrupulous investment partners, reckless real estate transactions, and other failures that I learned the lessons that finally stabilized my financial condition and fixed me upon a definite opinion about how to build wealth and manage one's finances.

Worst of all, I had all along thought I was being wise with my money, trying to do with it what "everyone" had always recommended. I didn't waste it on the proverbial "wine, women, and song" (I am happily married, hardly ever drink, and certainly can't sing!), but instead attempted to invest my money and grow it responsibly. Only then did I find out how much I still had to learn.

It turns out that nearly "everyone" is wrong when it comes to personal finances, and from that consideration grew the very concept of this book and its corresponding workbook.

Orrin's Story

Like Chris, I tried to follow the normal modern path to financial success by attempting to live my dreams through a good education and good job. In fact, I was working at General Motors and had developed several engineering patents when my life really changed. My wife Laurie and I argued a lot about finances because it seemed that there was never quite enough money to support our growing family.

I was enrolled in an MBA program at the University of Michigan at the time, and one evening after work as I was driving to class, I popped in an audiotape a friend had given me. What I heard over the next fifty minutes was a discussion about entrepreneurship, and I was so intrigued that I went looking for more tapes on the same subject.

Somewhere along the way, the ideas from the entrepreneurs on the tapes rubbed off on me, and I decided to take the leap and start my own business. It wasn't easy, but Laurie and I kept at it and over time began to achieve the financial success we wanted. But I still had a lot to learn about the principles of financial fitness.

In the process, I've helped found two multimillion-dollar companies and worked with some of the greatest people in this generation. It hasn't always been easy, but the results of the choice to take this path have been nothing less than amazing.

Over the years, as I have worked with many business associates and leaders, I have realized that most successful people follow a similar pattern. Few of us started out with a good understanding of financial principles, but those who achieve success learn our view of the principles of financial fitness and, more importantly, take action to apply these principles in their lives.

The results of learning the principles of financial fitness and applying them are always positive, and often they are truly spectacular.

Almost everyone has made mistakes with their personal finances, like I did, simply because they didn't know better. Many people received improper training on finances in their youth, and most young adults are average at best, or sometimes even terrible, at managing their money when they first leave home. Sadly, only a few people are significantly better at this even two or three decades later.

That is why this book can be such a help to so many people—because it outlines the principles of financial fitness that all of us should follow.

The Power of Principles

Between the two of us over the years, we have worked with hundreds and then thousands of people struggling to improve their finances, and we have seen time and again that a few simple changes make all the difference. In fact, it is amazing how little is really needed to turn things around and get on the path to financial fitness and prosperity.

In truth, the principles of financial fitness are not complex or difficult. Unfortunately, far too few learn these simple, basic principles that can fix their finances. Most people seem predisposed to stay in a rut unless something significant urges real change. If you live in a forest your whole life, you'll most likely think the world is made up of trees, just like a fish probably thinks the whole world is water. This reminds us of Plato's story about the prisoners locked up in a cave who just assume the whole world is a cave.

The same is true of understanding money. If your parents struggled with money and didn't know or apply the principles of financial fitness covered in this book, you most likely struggle as well. Some people learn the principles of money success by trial and error like we did, and some learn from mentors. But unless a person learns these principles and applies them in everyday life, he or she will continue to struggle financially.

Our schools seldom teach these principles, and it is difficult to find them all in the various books on the topic. Though there are a lot of writings on personal finance, including many that teach some of these principles of financial fitness, it is difficult for readers to plow through dozens of books just to find a principle here and another there.

The principles of financial success are relatively few and simple, but we haven't been able to find them effectively and thoroughly taught in one place in a way that truly helps people get their financial house in order. In fact, nearly all books now available on the topic fall into one of three categories:

1. Books on financial "offense" that explain how to make money, like the works of Robert Kiyosaki and David Bach and the many books on investing, entrepreneurship, and real estate.

2. Books on financial "defense" that explain how to save, budget, and get out of debt, like the writings of Dave Ramsey, Suze Orman, and dozens of others on overcoming debt.

3. Books on the "playing field," or the "rules" and "philosophy," of finance that explain how money works and how to understand economics, like titles by Ludwig von Mises, Peter Schiff, and Murray Rothbard.

But there is a great need for a single book that adequately teaches all three of these viewpoints and the skills of each because readers who get too caught up in offense will make drastic mistakes on the defensive side of things, while others who emphasize defense will limit their potential by not taking important offensive actions to increase their prosperity.

Those who focus mostly on the playing field, or the rules and philosophy approach, will have a good understanding of tax policy, the gold standard, or the benefits of a 401(k) but little real control over their financial goals.

We need to learn financial offense *and* defense, which can be summarized as "earning like a millionaire and living like the middle class." Too many people do the opposite and earn like the middle class but use debt to spend like they have a lot more than they do. The financially fit, in contrast, spend a lot less than they make. Sadly, few people in modern society consistently apply the principles of financial success.

Given this combination of improper training in regards to money, bad habits learned from many parents and friends, and the difficulty of finding classes or books that completely cover the full topic, many people are managing their finances in a way that resembles a hiker trying to find the right trails while unwittingly using the wrong map. No matter how hard he tries to study the map and follow it with precision, he is locked in to failure until he figures out what is wrong and gets a map that accurately reflects the territory.

True Financial Fitness

Many people want to live the principles of financial fitness, and they want to teach the tools of success to their children. Chris's wife Terri shared the story of their five-year-old daughter who was at lunch with friends. The woman who took them to lunch asked the little girl if she wanted a soda pop with her food. The girl immediately asked, "Is the drink included with the meal?"

Even at five years old, she understood the concept of value— at least to the point that she was only going to get the drink if it made financial sense. Of course, she didn't know all the details of financial offense and defense, but she had seen them modeled and knew the right question to ask.

In our society, so many people haven't seen the principles of financial fitness modeled. This makes it difficult to understand or apply them. People tend to do what they know based on their experience.

In this book, you will learn our view of the principles of financial success that brought us true financial fitness. This book combines all three approaches in one volume by outlining the key principles of financial success that we believe are necessary for a person or family to become financially fit.

This is truly a book on financial fitness. It is not a "get-rich" book, but rather a "get-fit" book, and there is a huge difference between these two approaches. Over time, those who are fit and follow the principles of financial success will attain prosperity and even wealth, but this comes from a long-term focus on doing the right things.

Fitness is a more clear parallel with happiness than "getting rich" is because being financially fit means living the kind of life that brings economic success but without unnecessary risk, complication, or a loss of focus on the more important things in life. It is a process, a lifestyle, a way of living, a set of values and good habits—not just a goal to be quickly attained and then forgotten. In fact, people who do get rich quick almost always lose their wealth because they aren't living the basic laws of financial fitness.

On a personal note, we feel so blessed that since those experiences on the Caribbean beach and listening to an audiotape while driving to a class, we've been able to learn the principles of financial fitness. Herein are the results of twenty years of wins and losses, gains and failures. Herein lies not advice, as we do not deign to advise anyone—everyone's situation being different. Instead, this book is for the purpose of education and to get the reader thinking about his or her true financial intelligence.

If we can, through these pages, impart some financial common sense, then our task will have been accomplished. We only wish this information had been available in this succinct form twenty years ago! May it be a blessing for you and save you from many wrong turns. Above all, may it help you get more financially fit and truly achieve your most important goals in life. We have learned that the principles of financial fitness work, and those who apply them *will* get financially fit.

BASICS

"THIS IS A FOOTBALL."

This is the most basic part of financial fitness, but instead of saying, "This is a football," "This is a basketball," or "This is a tennis racquet," as we would when discussing sports and physical fitness, we will introduce the equivalent in finances. Specifically, in Part I, we'll learn seven basic principles of financial fitness and how to implement them immediately. These seven principles and skills form the foundation for all financial success. The secret of success is to learn and *master* the basics!

We are what we repeatedly do. Excellence is therefore not an act but a habit.
—ARISTOTLE

We make a living by what we get, but we make a life by what we give.
—WINSTON CHURCHILL

Why Do Some People Have Plenty of Money, While Others Constantly Struggle Financially?

Annual income twenty pounds, annual expenditure nineteen six, result happiness. Annual income twenty pounds, annual expenditure twenty pound ought and six, result misery.
—FROM *DAVID COPPERFIELD* BY CHARLES DICKENS

W hy do some people have plenty of money, while others constantly struggle with their finances? Many people believe that wealth (or lack thereof) is a natural result of how a person was raised, but there are numerous examples of people who live far above, or below, the financial level of their parents.

Some who inherit great wealth waste and lose it, while others increase it. Some who inherit little or no money become very prosperous, while others do not.

Even within families, brothers and sisters grow up with a similar background and level of education, but some become affluent or even wealthy, while others consistently find it difficult to pay their bills. Clearly a person's inheritance or upbringing doesn't determine how financially successful he or she will become.

Another popular view is that education determines career and level of wealth, but while there is some correlation between levels of education and higher pay, every profession includes those with strong financial fitness and also many who are up to their eyeballs in debt.

The truth is that some janitors and taxi drivers follow the principles of financial fitness, and some do not. Likewise, some attorneys, bankers, CEOs, and doctors immerse themselves in debt and ignore the rules of financial success, while others do not. This applies to every career field and people from every walk of life.

We wrote in our book *LIFE:*

> Most people who make $30,000 per year believe if they made $40,000 per year their troubles would be over. Strangely, though, people who make $40,000 per year seem to believe it would take $50,000 per year to solve *their* problems. The trouble with this thinking is that no matter how much you make, if you spend it all, you're constantly at the financial cliff.

In other words, it's not what you make but what you keep that determines financial success. People can be financially solid making $30,000 per year. On the other hand, people can be financially insolvent making $500,000 per year. We have witnessed people in both positions numerous times over the years.[2]

IT'S NOT WHAT YOU MAKE BUT WHAT YOU KEEP THAT DETERMINES FINANCIAL SUCCESS. PAY YOURSELF FIRST AND SAVE WHAT YOU PAY YOURSELF.

There are many examples of this reality. Most people observing two families having a picnic at the park would assume that the family in the new Cadillac SUV and wearing designer-label clothes is more financially fit than the family in the older car and discount jeans and t-shirts.

But in our modern world, this is likely deceptive. The parents of the second family may make more money—*a lot* more—and may be much more able to afford the Cadillac and designer clothes than the first family. Indeed, the first family may be living on debt, while the second family carefully avoids it and focuses on savings and investments.

Learn the Principles

In short, there are principles of financial fitness. Those who understand and apply these proven principles see improved finances and eventually prosperity and even wealth, regardless of their background, education, or past experiences. In contrast, those who—for whatever reason—don't know or implement the principles of good financial fitness always struggle.

Financial fitness, like physical fitness, requires two things: knowing what to do and taking action to do it. For example, getting your body in shape is very difficult if you have the false belief that cupcakes, fast food, french fries, and candy bars are healthier than vegetables, fruits, lean meats and fish, and whole grains. If you think sitting on a couch is superior to quality exercise, you aren't likely to get fit any time soon.

Furthermore, just knowing what is healthy isn't enough. If you know that fast food and candy bars aren't as good for you as whole grains and vegetables but you stubbornly eat candy and pastries for most of your meals, or just skip meals and get by on stimulants like coffee or soft drinks, your other efforts to get healthier will likely suffer. If

> **Financial fitness, like physical fitness, requires two things: knowing what to do and taking action to do it.**

you know you should exercise but don't ever get around to it, you won't get your body in shape.

As we wrote in *Launching a Leadership Revolution*: "Everyone has an opinion about how to make improvements. Coming up with good ideas is no big deal. The world is full of great ideas and deep thinkers of grand theories. *Implementation and results make the difference. They separate the heroes from the rest.*"[3]

Becoming financially fit requires knowing what is financially healthy and then applying that knowledge. That's what this book is about. As you read, you will learn the principles that bring financial fitness, along with numerous skills and techniques for applying each one.

Real Power

Ultimately, your financial future is up to you. Just like physical fitness, your financial fitness is in your hands. You have the power to live your financial dreams, to get out of debt, to increase your income, to change old habits that have blocked your financial success, and to turn your financial weaknesses into strengths. This is a very exciting reality! To repeat: *You have the power to live your financial dreams, whatever they are.*

But without an accurate understanding of the principles of financial fitness, it is impossible to make real progress. No amount of discipline or personal willpower and not even a positive mental attitude can overcome a lack of knowledge; you must learn the principles of financial fitness in order to apply them.

The good news is that the principles you need are in this book and by applying them you will see success. There is great power in principles. Stephen Covey taught that principles are universal; meaning that when you apply them, you *know* you will get the results you seek.

For example, the law of the harvest teaches that you reap what you sow. If you plant wheat, you won't get a crop of corn; you'll get wheat. You have to water the wheat, weed it, keep animals from trampling it, and protect it from the weather if possible, but if you plant it and care for it, the law of the harvest tells you that you will get a wheat crop at the end of the growing season.

> **The reason that some people have enough money, while others constantly struggle financially, is simply because those people have learned the principles of financial fitness and consistently apply them—while others do not.**

The same is true of financial principles. You have to understand them, apply them, and follow them, and as you do, you can know with a surety that you will get your desired goals.

The reason that some people have enough money, while others constantly struggle financially, is simply because those people have learned the principles of financial fitness and consistently apply them—while others do not.

Our invitation to you is to be the exception, to become one of the few who understands and implements the principles of financial fitness. As you do this, you will not only help yourself, but you will create a legacy for your children, their children, and others you mentor in the principles of financial success.

CHAPTER TWO

Ascertaining What Money Really Means to You and Why It's Important to Be Financially Fit

Simple, genuine goodness is the best capital to found the business of this life upon. It lasts when fame and money fail, and is the only riches we can take out of this world with us.
—Louisa May Alcott

There is an old saying in business that example isn't the most important thing in leadership—it's the only thing. But money definitely isn't the only thing in life, nor is it even close to being the most important. Of the 8 Fs used in the LIFE Leadership system,[4] Finance isn't as important as Faith, Family, Freedom, Fitness (and health), or Friends, and many would argue that it isn't any more important than Fun or Following either.

But financial fitness holds a unique place in the list of things you should focus on in life because being financially fit can not only help you avoid the negative consequences, dread, and stress of being financially flabby (such as having poor credit and not being able to keep up with the bills, dealing with calls and letters from creditors, not being able to afford Christmas presents, fees for extracurricular activities for your children, not being able to properly maintain your home and automobiles, and so on), but it also hugely leverages how effective you can be in all of your life projects and endeavors. Without adequate finances, the potential of all of the roles, responsibilities, and relationships in your life is lessened.

When you are financially fit, you are able to do so much more for those you love and all those within your circles of influence. And being financially fit will also enable you to fund the pursuit of your dreams. Ultimately, it can even free you from the grind of exchanging your time and labor for money and allow you more time to passionately fulfill your purpose and live your dream.

However, there is a danger in focusing too much on money and making it the center of your life. Money certainly isn't everything, and the Bible is clear that an unbalanced focus on the love of money is the root of all evil. But too often, people misinterpret this as an excuse to let themselves become financially unfit.

God wants people to be financially fit, to live and apply the true principles of abundance He created. He wants everyone to experience the benefits of prosperity and the bounty of life. And most importantly, He wants people to use their resources to fulfill their calling in His Kingdom.

The Gift

Money is a gift. It has a specific use. This means that you have a stewardship. We humans are happiest and most successful when we use money for something that matters, for our families and beyond. The point of life is not to get good with money. It is important not to make the mistake of getting distracted by the wrong goals. Avoid getting fixated on money. Like a hammer, money is a *tool*, to be used to do the truly important things in life.

Indeed, money isn't the goal, but money can be a great, indispensable tool in achieving your true life goals, dreams, and purpose. Make money in order to

> **Make money in order to enable your priorities and build your stewardship.**

enable your priorities and build your stewardship. Taking your stewardship seriously does two things: 1) It fulfills your life purpose, and 2) It naturally brings in more money.

If you love Faith, Family, Freedom, and the other key parts of your life, financial fitness is necessary in order to live up to your potential. As mentioned, money is like a flashlight or a hammer; it is a tool that can be used to greatly support the things you love. Without financial fitness, your ability to do the things you care about most will always be diminished.

Start with the basics!

MONEY IS A GIFT. IT HAS A SPECIFIC USE. THIS MEANS THAT YOU HAVE A STEWARDSHIP. YOU ARE TO USE YOUR MONEY FOR SOMETHING THAT MATTERS, FOR YOUR FAMILY AND BEYOND.

The Importance of Time

In his book *A Month of Italy,* Chris shows how important spending enough time with your spouse and kids is to the well being of your family and marriage. We all honor the great men and women in our past or in the world who have sacrificed time away from their spouses and children in order to work long hours, often in multiple jobs, to support the needs of their family.

This is an honorable sacrifice, but there is an even better way available. Those who truly understand and consistently apply the principles of financial fitness can learn to effectively support their families in ways that allow them extra time to spend with their spouse, children, and extended family and friends—as well as to serve others.

The principles of financial fitness work because they are universal, and when they are applied, real success (the kind that includes time for what you value most) becomes not only possible but also inevitable.

A Look Inside

Try the following exercise. Imagine that today you receive a call or a letter notifying you that you have just inherited $10 million from a distant relative. You are surprised that this relative had so much money because she always seemed very normal to you, and you are even more surprised that she gave the money all to you. After verifying that the inheritance is true, not just some hoax from your prankster brother or cousin, you sit down to decide what you will do with the money.

It immediately dawns on you that this could change your life in many ways. Now answer the following questions as if this has really happened. First, what will you do with your work and career? How will you spend your time each day? What do you really want to spend your time doing for the rest of your life?

Some people think they would quit work and watch television, but for the few who have actually been able to do this, such a focus has proven very unfulfilling. So, seriously, what would you want to do with the years ahead? Would you stay in your current career? Switch to another? Build a business, or grow the one you already have?

Second, with whom do you want to spend more time, and what do you want to do with them? This is a hugely important question because it helps you see where your heart really is right now.

Next, what do you want to learn, experience, or do? Do you want to travel, learn to play a musical instrument or to speak another language, or pursue a higher education or some other interest? Do you want to make a lot more money? Make a list.

Fourth, how would you use some of your money in the Faith area of your life? What about Family? Fun? Freedom?

Finally, after you pay taxes on your inheritance, where do you want to donate some of your money—to a hospital, a school, your church, or somewhere else? This also helps you see where your heart really is and what you'd like to do to improve the world.

This is a profound question: What would you do to change the world if you could?

We wrote in *Launching a Leadership Revolution*: "Everybody seems to have an innate sense that something is needed. It is not hard to identify problems in a given situation. Ask people to identify what's wrong with their church, employer, or neighbors, and you'd better be prepared for a long explanation. Don't even get them started on the government! That could take days."[5]

There is so much that the world needs, and some of it intersects with your passions and interests. There are three things that you can do with your money:

> **What would you do to change the world if you could?**

1. Acquire (things)
2. Accomplish (goals and dreams)
3. Contribute (to causes and people in need)

If you had the time and resources, what would you contribute to help improve the world in important ways? Take the time to write down your answers to each of the questions above.

What's Ahead for You?

Now look over your answers and ask yourself how more money could help you live your dreams and help others.

In the real world, you may or may not receive such an inheritance, but instead of holding your breath until it happens, simply understand that by living the principles of financial fitness, you can build financial reservoirs that will enable you to live your dreams. It takes time, but five, ten, or twenty years from now, you'll either be five, ten, or twenty years older and financially in the same place you are today, or you'll be five, ten, or twenty years older and financially fit. It's up to you.

It all depends on how effectively you learn and apply the principles of financial fitness. Everyone can be financially fit, if they understand and implement the principles.

THREE

How to Begin Getting Financially Fit

Money isn't everything....But it ranks right up there with oxygen.
—RITA DAVENPORT

We have all been there. We look in the mirror and realize that we've gotten out of shape and get inspired to get fit again. It's time to put on our running shoes and renew the gym membership. We pull out the old gym bag, pencil out an exercise plan, and go jogging. The next day, we get up early and lift weights.

Later that afternoon, we realize we have made a serious mistake—two mistakes, in fact. First, we forgot to stretch before we went running (which was mostly walking, as it turned out). Second, we forgot to stretch out again before and after we lifted weights. As the evening progresses, we feel increasingly sore.

By the next morning, our aching muscles are screaming at us, "Don't do any more exercise! This hurts! This is crazy. Just eat less or something."

We pay attention to this voice (something we have rarely done over the past months as we let our eating habits get out of control and got out of shape). So today, instead of exercise, we go to a used bookstore and browse through the diet books. We find one that looks promising, buy it, and put ourselves on a new regimen. Or we skip the diet book and just try to improve our habits and eat less on our own.

In our new focus on healthy food, we realize just how often we have been taking the extra cookie or fitting in one more late-night snack. But three days later, our family members are walking around us on emotional eggshells as we become increasingly short-tempered.

This goes on for a few days, and by the end of two weeks, most of us are back to the old, normal plan—the unhealthy one.

The Ritual Financial Fix

Even if you have never personally gone through this popular North American fitness ritual, you have almost certainly experienced its closest cousin: the "fix my finances" plan.

First, a book, an audio download, a friend, or a pile of overdraft notices and bills you couldn't pay probably inspired you. Next, you went cold turkey and stopped spending and threatened your spouse and children to get them to do the same. Then you lamented the amount of taxes withheld from your salary and the limits of your paycheck.

If you are married, you likely had some fights about finances with your spouse. If you are single, you probably still fought with your roommates about who owed how much on the cable bill.

Finally, after a long stretch of not spending anything and lecturing your spouse on his or her spending habits, you finally broke down and splurged on a big $450 purchase you didn't really need. But somehow it made you feel better for a few hours. Then, inevitably, you started over at the beginning of this cycle and repeated the pattern.

A Better Way

In this book, we are going to suggest that you never follow this plan again. To the contrary, you need to do things right this time. Real change lasts, and it is time for *real change*.

In truth, as we discussed in earlier chapters, your finances are flabby if you aren't following the principles of financial fitness. Instead of going on a crash financial diet or an extreme money exercise plan, you need to understand and simply begin to apply the principles of financial success.

So, it's time to ask yourself a very important question. In earlier chapters, you've already learned two principles of financial health:

PRINCIPLE 1: It's not what you make but what you keep that determines financial success. Pay yourself first and save what you pay yourself.

PRINCIPLE 2: Money is a gift. It has a specific use. This means that you have a stewardship. You are to use your money for something that matters, for your family and beyond.

Here is the key, life-changing question: What have you done to apply these two principles since you read them?

Be Transformational

For most people, reading is an informational process. We read to learn things, and long years in school have taught us that learning means understanding and remembering. After all, if we held a pop quiz right now and asked what the first two principles listed in this book are, nearly every reader could list and explain both.

But to become financially fit, you need to embrace a different kind of learning. Instead of just doing *informational* reading, you need to become a *transformational* reader. You need to read each principle of financial fitness in this book with an eye toward application. It isn't enough to simply understand a principle; you must *implement* it in everyday life.

43

Every time you learn a new principle of financial fitness in this book, stop reading and figure out how you will apply it in your life—for real. This is what we call "being a hero,"[6] being the kind of person who goes beyond information and ideas and actually takes action!

> Instead of just doing *informational* reading, you need to become a *transformational* reader. It isn't enough to simply understand a principle; you must *implement* it in everyday life.

Prioritize Your Spending

How can you apply Principle 1? How do you keep more of what you make? Imagine that you are a company called YOU, Inc. and that, along with all of your other creditors, you are in line trying to get your bill paid. If you prioritize all of your various bills in order of importance, the YOU, Inc. bill should be at the front of the line. You need to pay yourself first.

Paying yourself first is analogous to putting your oxygen mask on first before trying to help anyone else when in an emergency situation while flying on an airplane. If you don't take care of yourself first, you will not be of much use to anyone else. And if you don't pay yourself first, you will have more trouble keeping up with your other expenses, let alone ever getting ahead and funding your dreams and life purpose.

Step one to paying yourself first is to open a savings account. If you already have a savings account, open another one for this step. This account should be treated as sacred, as it will create the capital you need to eventually take you from survival to success.

Step two is to create a plan for consistently adding money to this account. Each time you get paid from now on, pay yourself 10% of your income into this account. It's only 10%, but it will grow your savings and net worth more quickly than you might think.

44

You might doubt that you can pay all your bills if you are putting away 10%, but we have never seen anyone who couldn't make it happen. We have seen people cut their cable bill, reduce their soft drink purchases, get a second job or start a business in the evenings, and do a whole host of other things in order to grow their savings.

If you want your finances to change, you are going to need to change something about your finances. These two steps will make all the difference in your financial life and put you on the path to financial fitness.

People who don't keep some of the money they make are never financially successful. George S. Clason wrote in *The Richest Man in Babylon*: "Gold cometh gladly and in increasing quantity to any man who will put by not less than one-tenth of his earnings to create an estate for his future and that of his family."[7]

By keeping 10% each time you get paid, you immediately begin breaking the old financial habits that have held you back and learn to live below your means consistently.

These actions are your first baby steps toward financial fitness. Statistics predict that not everyone who reads this chapter will actually stop and do both of these now, but those who do will be on their way to true financial fitness. Be the exception; be one of those who stops and does both steps right away.

Actually, we hope *every* reader does these two powerful steps. They are really much more than baby steps because they will switch your financial direction from one of struggles to getting financially fit. Stop and do both of these steps right now. Be the kind of learner who takes immediate action when you learn a new principle. And follow the same pattern for the rest of this book.

YOU, Inc.

The value of a company is determined by looking at its current income and assets and at its ability to compete in future markets and economic shifts. How much would the stock of your company YOU, Inc. be valued at today? Are you a blue-chip stock or a penny stock? If you're not yet a blue-chip stock, it's likely because your company is underfunded and in debt and its management lacks the leadership and financial education to compete in today's marketplace. This is why it is so important for you to invest in YOU, Inc. Consider this as sacred as your purpose and invest at least 10% of your income as seed money to enable YOU, Inc. to grow and prosper.

We developed a very simple and predictable formula to help people transform their penny stocks into blue-chips called the YOU, Inc. Investment Hierarchy. This hierarchy prioritizes all of the various investment categories in order of importance. Later in the book, we will review each level of the hierarchy in depth, explaining the types of investments and their significance.

The first and most important level of the hierarchy is investing in yourself—by investing in your personal development and financial and leadership education, expanding your ability and capacity to perform, and investing in entrepreneurial or intrapreneurial activities. Benjamin Franklin wrote, "If a man empties his purse into his head, no man can take it away from him. An investment in knowledge always pays the best interest." By investing in this financial program, you are filling in the foundation of your first hierarchy level.

Remember, your financial future is in *your* hands. You are the most important investment there is, and you do have the power to live your financial dreams, whatever they are.

Your Long-Term Vision

Now that you have a new savings account and a plan to increase it every time you get paid, how are you applying Principle 2? Specifically, what is your stewardship? What is your mission in life? What is your long-term vision and dream? What do you want to do with your life stewardship? And how much money will you need to effectively accomplish your dreams and plans?

Take the time to answer these questions in writing. Unlike the fictional exercise earlier in this book about inheriting $10 million, this time your answers to the questions are real. This is your life. What do you want to do with it?

Take your stewardship seriously and fully write out your answers to the questions above. Write your long-term vision and dream. This matters. Knowing your stewardship, to your family and beyond, is an essential part of financial fitness. Knowing what you want to do with your life and how much money you want and need in order to accomplish your goals is a vital part of getting in financial shape.

If you don't have a long-term vision, your money will naturally get frittered away. Successful people have a written financial plan. We want you to be financially successful, so write out your vision.

What do you want to do, what do you want to spend your money on, and how much money do you want to spend on your stewardship? Give real effort and time to answering these questions in writing.

Again, you can be an informational reader and simply read these words without taking action, or you can be a *transformational* learner and leader by actually applying the principles of financial success. Only those who stop and implement the principles of financial fitness will build the habits and legacy of long-term money success.

Amazingly, as we said earlier, the principles of financial fitness aren't difficult or complex. They are actually quite simple. But like Naaman in the Bible, who was told to heal his leprosy simply by bathing several times in the river and resisted the advice because it seemed too simple or silly, too many people just read informationally and do not take the time to stop and do the exercises that will make them financially fit.

These assignments are *so simple*. Do them! If you have skipped any to this point, go back and do every one. This is such a small thing, yet it will yield huge positive results in your financial life. The accompanying workbook will help you in this very important process and make these tasks even easier. Do not miss this opportunity to do the small things that will drastically increase your financial success.

FOUR

More on How to Begin Getting Financially Fit

A penny saved is a penny earned.
—BENJAMIN FRANKLIN

Benjamin Franklin started his life broke, but he created wealth by first working for a wage and saving every penny he could, all the while intentionally planning for and taking action on achieving his dreams.

Once Franklin had money, fame, and the time to do whatever he wanted, he kept writing and spreading his influence. He helped many other people understand the principles of success, and he dedicated much of his time to the freedom of his young nation.

He taught that the key to financial success is to live within your means. This simple concept is seldom followed, and those who don't follow it always struggle financially.

LIVE WITHIN YOUR MEANS. ALWAYS. NO EXCEPTIONS. PERIOD. FOLLOW A GOOD BUDGET. GIVE EACH SPOUSE A SMALL ALLOWANCE SO YOU HAVE A LITTLE DISCRETIONARY MONEY EACH MONTH, AND DON'T NITPICK EACH OTHER ON THE LITTLE THINGS.

Take Action

How are you going to apply this simple yet vital principle? First, make a good budget. Sit down, outline all your income and expenses, and create a workable budget. Successful people do this, and people who don't are financially out of shape. If you are married, get on the same page with your spouse in this process.

List all your income and expenses for at least the last six months. Only list actual income, not "if-come" that you *hope* to receive. Include irregular, periodic expenses like home or car repairs. And be sure to include the costs of paying for your debts. Don't exaggerate income or discount your expenses. Be accurate. If anything, overestimate your expenses—to account for rising costs and inflation, and just to be safe.

Find out your *net* cash flow, the difference between your income and expenses. If your expenses are higher than your income, then you are broke. Our government has a hard time with this, and so do the majority of people. The government may be able to get away with it for a while, but you can't.

Now, once you have real data in front of you, figure out an effective budget. Be realistic. Cut things that should be cut. And plan on remaking your budget monthly since every month is different.

One great technique to help you stay within your budget is using the cash envelope system. Each time you get paid, put the allotted cash amount for each budgeted item in a separate envelope. This helps prevent overspending.

If you want to buy an item that costs more than what is in the envelope, you have three options: 1) Put off the purchase until you have enough in the envelope, 2) Purchase something less expensive, or 3) Purchase the item and transfer money from another envelope to cover the cost. All three choices will still allow you to live within your means. If you make the third choice and you are married, make sure both spouses are in agreement regarding changes to any part of the previously agreed upon budget.

With the cash envelope system, you can easily set aside money for irregular, periodic expenses ahead of time. For example, if you estimate that your yearly auto maintenance/repair expenses are $2,400, you would put $200 per month in that envelope.

There are various great materials available that help you with creating a budget and cash flow management plan, especially the workbook that goes along with this book. If you haven't started using the workbook yet, now is a great time to do so. The workbook will make budgeting much easier and help you ask the right questions.

Second, follow your budget. Use discipline and plan ahead. Write down all of your income, savings, and expenses, and "spend" your income on paper before you actually use any of it. Become the master of your money and closely track every financial transaction.

A wise mentor once counseled a man about his financial struggles, and the man said he couldn't make and follow a budget because it always led to fights with his wife. The mentor asked him if he really loved his wife. "Of course, I do," the man assured him.

"Then it is time to fight," the mentor declared. "Some fights are worth having, and a real budget is essential to success. Be loving, positive, and patient," he told his mentee, "but work out a budget with your wife and follow it. In the long term, it will save your relationship."

Equally profound advice is to stop listening to your broke friends and relatives and their bad financial opinions. If they are broke, their financial counsel isn't worth the time it takes to listen to them. Shut off the gobbledygook of the 95% who don't know what they are talking about.[8]

A lot of people are upside down on their mortgage (many even with a second mortgage), upside down on their cars, have huge credit card debt, and don't have much stuff to show for all their spending. Their lack of discipline has made them an asset for their bank.

Only listen to financial mentors who actually have their finances in a state you want to emulate.

STOP GETTING FINANCIAL ADVICE FROM BROKE PEOPLE; GET IT ONLY FROM THOSE WHOSE FINANCES YOU WANT TO EMULATE.

If you find yourself struggling to follow a budget, get a good financial advisor to help you and hold you accountable.

The List

Now, take a few minutes and make a list of people you have listened to on financial topics. Include family, friends, relatives, influential teachers, etc.

Once you have completed the list, use your pen or pencil to cross out every person whose finances you would not want to emulate. Circle those whose finances you would like to emulate.

From now on, weigh all financial advice using this same criterion. Keep this list and add to it over time as you hear counsel on finances from additional people.

Prepare Ahead

Next, add an emergency fund to your budget. Murphy's Law predicts that unexpected expenses will come up. Even if you don't believe in this law, being prepared for the unexpected is wise counsel. The dog may get sick (probably from eating all that homework), the house may need sudden major repairs, a fender bender may send your car to the shop, or a car transmission might need to be replaced. Budget for these expenses and others like them ahead of time.

Investing in your emergency fund is Level Two of the YOU, Inc. Investment Hierarchy. Have the discipline to pay yourself first and fill in the hierarchy. The goal is to get the account up to $1,000 as soon as possible. Do whatever it takes to get this done quickly! This will help you withstand some bumps in the road that may come along. It will also naturally help you start thinking differently and seeing your finances from a more secure perspective.

And then work on increasing your emergency fund to the point where it will cover three to six months of your living expenses. Protect this fund and don't ever touch it unless you experience a true emergency. A vacation or that new television on sale is *not* an emergency! But when you encounter experiences like the time your washer broke, flooded the entire basement, and ruined all your luggage just before the big family trip, you will be ready to respond with minimal hardship.

Nobody really wants such unexpected expenses, but emergencies are inevitable. However, those with an emergency fund handle them with very little effort or concern. Being prepared provides great peace of mind in times of trouble. And having a special account specifically dedicated to your emergency fund will make you less likely to spend from it frivolously.

CONSISTENTLY BUDGET AND SAVE FOR UNEXPECTED EXPENSES.

Be sure to take action on all three of the principles covered in this chapter. These, along with the two principles listed earlier, are among the most basic and immediate things each person can do to quickly transition from financial flabbiness to financial fitness.

Master the Basics

Note that of the five principles we have covered so far, the first two apply to offense (getting more money), while the next three belong to the defense category (protecting against debt and loss). But all of them are basics of financial fitness.

The key to success in any field is to master the basics. The great basketball player Larry Bird made this idea popular by exemplifying this principle. Even as one of the best NBA players who ever lived, he stayed long after practice nearly every day working on dribbling, layups, and the most basic skills of the game.

By mastering the simple, basic financial skills covered so far in this book, you are establishing a solid and lasting foundation for true financial fitness. The basics of financial fitness may too seem simple to make a big difference, but those who do them find financial success.

In contrast, those who don't do the basics never quite seem to understand why others get ahead financially while they are still struggling.

Open the savings account and fund it with 10% of your income each month. Stop listening to the wrong financial advice. Take the time to build a good budget and then follow it. Get on the path to financial success.

This book is about taking action, not long discussions of philosophy that seldom get followed or implemented. Half of reading this book is about learning and understanding what is written; the other half is all about stopping and applying each principle by completing every assignment. Both of these are extremely important.

FIVE

How to Change Your Financial Habits

You miss one hundred percent of the shots you never take.
—WAYNE GRETZKY

Change is hard for most people. Self-discipline is one of the most challenging lessons for any of us to learn. When it comes to finances, this can be especially difficult. But financial fitness is the natural result of applying the basic principles of financial success. Those who do these simple things will become financially fit, and eventually they will be financial powerhouses. We want you to be among them!

Success is simple. Learn and follow the principles of financial fitness. The hardest part for most people is simply getting started. But learning from the examples of many others who have made the switch from financial weakness to true financial fitness helps.

> **Success is simple. Learn and follow the principles of financial fitness. The hardest part for most people is simply getting started.**

Dan and Lisa Hawkins's Story

Warren Buffett is one of the wealthiest people in the world. He created his wealth through wise investment strategies compounded over time. In a CNBC interview, Warren Buffett gave advice to college students. Not surprisingly, his advice is spot on for helping people get out of the Financial Matrix:

> CNBC: "What is the one thing that young people should be doing about money?"
> Buffett: "I tell them two things, generally. One is **stay away from credit cards**.…The second thing I tell them is to **invest in themselves**."

In a nutshell, his advice breaks out into two categories: 1) Live debt-free, and 2) Invest in yourself. First, learn the defense of finances to get out of debt, and then invest the savings to go on offense in the number one asset you have, namely, yourself. Buffett, perhaps the greatest investment manager of all time, emphasized the importance of self-investment when he asked a group of college students if they would take $50,000 cash for 10% of their future pay. When nearly half the students raised their hands to accept the offer, Buffett pointed out that they must be worth at least $500,000 since 10% of $500,000 is $50,000. Then he drove the message home by asking the students how many other $500,000 assets they currently had. Of course, all the hands went down. *You*, in other words, are your greatest return on investment. Period.

After a slow start, Dan and Lisa Hawkins took this advice to heart. It seemed like every time they attempted to go on offense, the lack of capital hindered their efforts. To use a football analogy, they never seemed to get on offense because their defense never let the offense on the playing field. Through mentorship, however, Dan and Lisa got serious about debt reduction. Although they were only making $50,000 per year combined, they wiped out debt quickly by applying the proper financial principles. For instance, Dan had been spending $8–10 on vending machine snacks and drinks with another $5–10 for lunch every day. These were quickly cut, and Dan began packing a lunch from home and curtailing his soda pop consumption on the job. In addition, Dan and Lisa canceled their cable subscription and began to read more, and they stopped spending on movies and restaurant meals. They put the money saved from cutting expenses toward investing in business training materials.

Gaining confidence in practicing delayed gratification, Dan sold his hot rod Mustang and paid cash for a $3,000 replacement vehicle. He then used the remaining cash to pay off Lisa's car and effectively eliminated $600 of monthly payments through applying the proper financial principles. Dan and Lisa paid off one credit card and then another, and over a couple of years, they eliminated two car loans, several credit card balances, an ATV loan, a computer loan, student loans, and finally their mortgage!

Dan and Lisa disciplined themselves to follow four simple principles:

1. When you receive income, immediately put 10% toward tithing and 10% toward savings.
2. Then, minimize expenses (self-entertainment) and maximize investments (self-education).
3. Then, pay the minimum payments on your debts and put any extra from cutting expenses toward the balance of your highest interest rate debt aside from your home.
4. After the first three items are done, pay the rest of your bills.

Once the process was rolling, the victories achieved created momentum for future successful outcomes. Not surprisingly, thanks to the disciplined approach to finances, the Hawkins family eventually accumulated thousands of dollars in savings.

With their business income continuing to grow and all debt eliminated, their nest egg grew rapidly. This allowed them the freedom to purchase a house three times as big as their previous one with a substantial down payment. As they built up their savings, they retired debt and used the greater cash flow to increase investment in themselves and their growing business. Newer cars and better vacations followed as the Hawkins family lived a cash lifestyle in which they only spent money they had already earned. Still, they kept saving a portion of all income. Amazingly, through increases in their business and financial discipline, the Hawkins family went on to buy an 8,500-square-foot custom home on over twenty acres, paying almost 50% equity at closing. Dreams do come true for those who read, listen to, learn, and apply the timeless principles of financial fitness.

Today, the Hawkinses lead a multimillion-dollar leadership company and speak across North America teaching financial and leadership principles to others. By following Warren Buffett's two key wealth-building principles of getting out of debt and investing in themselves, Dan and Lisa Hawkins went from living in dread to living their dreams.

Techniques for Effective Change

Everyone must eventually make the choice to become an adult where finances are concerned. The sooner you do it, the easier it usually is. Also, there are several powerful techniques that can help you increase your financial discipline.

As with the principles of financial fitness in this book, make each of the following techniques part of your change to true financial success by thinking about ways to put them into action. Then write down your plans and implement them!

1. One of the biggest problems that keep people from improving their financial habits is coming across what seems like an exceptional deal. This can blow the budget and get you off track.

This frequently happens while a person is shopping and a deal that is "too good to pass up" presents itself. For example:

When Misty returned home from shopping, she quickly lifted the cardboard box from the trunk and hid it in the garage so nobody would notice. After the twins emptied the trunk and put all the groceries away, she sighed in relief that her plan had worked. Then she forgot about the box.

The next weekend Derrick walked into the kitchen carrying the box. "I was tidying up," he said, "and I came across this box. What is it?"

Misty decided to just be honest. "Uh, well, when I went grocery shopping on Thursday, I saw a big yard sale and stopped to see what they had. I know we agreed not to spend money on anything beyond our budget, but they had so many cute things. I just couldn't help myself."

Derrick shook his head and placed the box on the table. "Well, let's see what you got," he said pleasantly. The first thing in the box was a pair of toddler shoes. Derrick stared at them in amazement, and then a smile slowly crept across his face. "Tom, Jade," he called loudly, "come down to the kitchen for a minute."

When the twins arrived, he held the shoes up to Tom's large teenage feet. "These don't fit Tom," he announced. Misty knew she was being teased, and she began laughing as Derrick held the tiny shoes up to Jade's feet and shook his head in mock disappointment. "They don't fit Jade either, honey," he said.

"Maybe they will fit me," he said hopefully as he compared the small shoes to his size twelve feet. "Nope. Well, will they fit you, dear?" Misty was laughing so hard now that tears began running down her cheeks. The twins joined her when they realized what was going on.

"Boy, they don't fit anyone in our family," Derrick said in a puzzled voice. "I'm sure glad you bought them, though. I mean, they're sooooooo cute."

It is amazing how often people buy things just because they seem like such a great deal at the moment. The key is to hold yourself to the 24 Hour Rule: If you ever see a deal that is just too good to be true, wait twenty-four hours before you buy. It will save you a lot of money over time. Even if it looks like you'll lose out on the deal, in the long run, sticking to the 24 Hour Rule will be a huge blessing.

Learn to wait and deny yourself. There will always be another deal, but sticking to your budget is the best deal of all.

> **There will always be another deal, but sticking to your budget is the best deal of all.**

As you attain more wealth, you can amend the 24 Hour Rule by putting a price on it. For example, Orrin uses $500, and if he wants to buy something that costs more, he waits at least twenty-four hours. Until you have wealth, your number should be very small. At first, just apply the 24 Hour Rule to all purchases.

Do not make spontaneous purchases. They are not okay. They are one of the biggest temptations when we are trying to live within our means. As Benjamin Franklin taught about finances, even a very small leak can sink a big ship.

Too many people are shopaholics and refuse to admit it. The level of your shopaholism is directly determined by how often you make spontaneous purchases—big or small. If you have this problem, admit it and stop doing it if you want to be financially fit. Getting your finances in order is completely worth it compared to the short-term high of a spontaneous buy.

2. Have an emergency fund, as discussed earlier. Note that your emergency fund is not for Christmas or good deals or other savings. It is only for true emergencies. Don't touch it for any other purpose.

3. As we also covered earlier, pay yourself first and keep that money always. Do not ever spend it. This is a strange concept for most people because they have been raised without understanding the principles of financial fitness. But this is a key part of financial success. In later chapters, we will talk about advanced places to put some of this savings. But for now, just get a separate savings account, pay 10% of everything you make to this account, and leave it there.

4. Create automatic transfers that build this fund monthly or every time you receive income. Making this automatic is a huge help. You won't even notice it going every month, and you won't have to make the monthly decision to transfer it yourself. Make Principle 1 (paying yourself) automatic!

Techniques for Effective Financial Discipline

5. If you are really struggling to make these changes (and unless you pay off your full credit card bill every single month), cut up your credit cards. Or freeze them in ice and leave them in the freezer so that if you come to a moment of weakness, you will have to wait for them to thaw. (If you microwave them, they will be ruined.) Somehow having to hand over cash for a purchase hurts more than just scanning a credit card.

6. In the same vein, set it up so that if you want to withdraw money from your bank, your financial mentor has to give approval and/or be present—especially for spontaneous purchases or uses of your emergency fund. This will make you stop and

think about whether or not you really need this purchase. Whatever you decide, you'll also have to convince your mentor.

7. Keep close track of everything you spend. This is an important habit. This really matters. Write every penny you spend in a notebook, frequently add up the totals, and discuss them with your partner. Keeping an eye on your money will help you get control of it. See the workbook for assistance with tracking tools.

8. If you are struggling with debt, communicate closely with your creditors. As long as you are paying them something, you are their asset. You can call and negotiate with them. There are companies out there that can negotiate for you, but some are scam artists, so be sure to check them out before engaging their services. Also note that some of them have high fees, so be careful.

But communicate with those to whom you owe money and negotiate so they will keep working with you. They want you to keep paying them, so if you work with them, they are usually motivated to make deals.

9. Renting a house can be a good idea for some people, especially when the economy is down because you won't have to ride a downward valuation slide. Also, this will save you the many costs of maintaining a home. People think owning a home is the only way to go, but in a struggling economy, the opposite is often true (more on this later).

10. If needed, sell some of your stuff. This can feel hard at the time, but it helps get your mind in the right place when you sacrifice to achieve your new goals of financial fitness. For example, in a lean year, Chris searched through the garage and sold some old motocross trading cards. In fact, online he sold one small pack of cards for $60 and an old book on Ford Mustangs for $90. This was a real blessing in a time of financial struggles. Whether you sell online or at a garage sale, just find things sitting around and sell them.

More Essential Techniques

11. Give yourself rewards for meeting your goals, such as going out to a movie if you stay within the budget all week. Use simple rewards and hold yourself to them.

For example, Rob spent his sophomore summer of college selling door to door. He had been offered a business internship. But a mentor told him that gaining sales experience would be among the most important things he could do, so he found himself in the hot Midwestern sun and humidity walking from house to house trying to sell.

He made $26,000 in three months, so the next summer, he decided to do the same thing again. This time he was a veteran, and he hit the first day of sales and every day afterward fired up and working hard.

The second year, he smiled happily every time his presentation was rejected and positively entered another checkmark on his page. He knew from his records of the past year that he had averaged nineteen rejections for every purchase, so he worked hard to get nineteen marks on his sheet.

When he marked off rejection ten, he said aloud, "This is so exciting. I'm more than halfway to a sale!" When he marked off the sixteenth rejection, he walked faster with anticipation. "Only three more to paydirt!" he told himself enthusiastically.

His increased energy made him a better salesman, and he found that this year, he made a sale for every thirteen rejections. Still, it was extremely hard work, so he motivated himself with a sheet showing the reward he would get at the end of the summer. He promised himself a small used car if he made over $30,000 and a Mustang if he earned over $70,000. The ultimate reward, what he *really* wanted, was a Toyota Tundra truck with a crew cab, which he promised himself if he sold over $100,000 during the summer.

When he returned to school with his new truck and over $100,000 in the bank (he had earned over $130,000 in three months), he told his friends that at the end, he kind of wanted to just bank the money and skip the truck.

"But then part of me kept telling myself, 'You pushed yourself to be out selling by 9:00 a.m. every day and to keep selling until after 9:00 p.m. every night for months, and the whole time, you opened your folder and admired pictures of that new, gray Toyota Tundra. If you don't honor your promise to yourself, you'll never be that kind of salesman again.'"

Inspire yourself and honor your promises to yourself. Of course, it is best to start with small, simple rewards and build up over time. For example, the first summer, Rob rewarded himself by eating out at his favorite restaurant for every six sales that he made.

> **Inspire yourself and honor your promises to yourself.**

12. Pay 10% of your income to tithing and give generously to charity and philanthropy. The spirit of giving is the spirit of abundance, and living in the attitude of abundance will bless you in many ways. That said, don't give to charity with the thought that by giving you will receive more. It can happen that way, but don't expect it. Give to help. Give even if you are really broke.

Financial guru Suze Orman suggests that if you are scared or worried about your finances, the first thing you should do is write out a check to charity and send it. If you are really worried, send several checks. This puts you in an abundant frame of mind and helps you view your financial concerns from a better perspective. Someone is much worse off than you are, and C. S. Lewis said that the right amount to give is enough that it pinches.

Do not send money you don't have, but cancel your cable, stop going to Starbuck's for coffees, or sell something and give to those who need it even more than you do.

PAY 10% OF YOUR INCOME TO TITHING. GIVE EVEN IF YOU ARE REALLY BROKE. GIVING PUTS YOU IN A MINDSET OF ABUNDANCE AND PUTS ANY FINANCIAL WORRIES IN THEIR PROPER PERSPECTIVE, SO IT SHOULD NOT BE LIMITED TO JUST TITHING. THE BIBLE CATEGORIZES GIVING AS: 1) TITHES AND 2) OFFERINGS.

Chris likes to tell the story of a friend's little brother who put his clip-on tie in the offering plate when he was a child. He thought the pastor said, "Ties and offerings." His heart was in the right place, and he was following Principle 6 even at that young age!

13. Know your purpose in life. Don't let money or the complications that come with it clutter your life. Focus on the goose that lays the golden eggs, meaning your work or business or other source of income (we will learn more about this later), and not so much on what to do with the eggs. Even if some opportunity is a great financial deal, if it takes away from your life purpose, do not get stuck with it.

14. Both spouses need to be on board. This is extremely important. In many relationships, one person is the natural spender, and the other is a natural saver. Do what it takes to work together to become financially fit.

If your marriage is like that of Jane Bennett and Mr. Bingley in Jane Austen's classic book *Pride and Prejudice*, meaning that both spouses are natural spenders, it is especially important to get the help of a good financial mentor who can hold you accountable. Otherwise, someone may write a book about you someday, too!

Stay Positive

In all this, find ways to make it fun. Learning and applying the principles of financial fitness should be enjoyable. The truth is that control over your finances will make you feel happier, stronger, more confident, and more in control of other facets of your life. When people begin to feel control over their money, they nearly always comment on how much the other areas of their life seem to improve.

Take the time to feel the benefits of these positive changes as they are occurring. As you talk to your spouse or others about these financial adjustments, focus on the positives. Business researcher Peter Drucker found that a common theme with great leaders is that they nearly always "starve the problems and feed the opportunities." Applying the principles in this book and using the workbook to help you record progress and focus on building consistently will help you stay positive.

Moreover, be proud of yourself as you make these changes in your life. This is hard work, but you are up to the challenge. And you will see your character increase along with your prosperity as you gain the habits of financial fitness. You can do this!

SIX

Once You Have Started Doing the Basics, What's Next?

Success is neither magical nor mysterious.
Success is the natural consequence of consistently
applying the basic fundamentals.
—JIM ROHN

Once you are doing the basics, master the basics! This wise counsel can apply to many fields, and perhaps all, but it is especially relevant to financial fitness. In Part II of this book, we will present the financial fitness principles of offense (how to make more money), and then in Part III, we will focus on defense (how to take care of and protect your money). But the preliminary basics we are covering now are the *foundation* of financial success.

Money and Happiness

Another important basic principle of financial fitness deals with the relationship between finances and happiness. *The Declaration of Independence* lists life, liberty, and the pursuit of happiness as three of the most important inalienable rights enjoyed by all human beings. While life and freedom are obviously needed for financial success, the pursuit of happiness is equally vital.

We need an environment of liberty in order to be able to dream, grow, achieve, and increase in prosperity.

However, happiness is not entirely tied to money. People can be happy without prosperity, and in fact, some great heroes have proven that it is possible to be happy even without freedom. But when people have money problems, it nearly always negatively influences their feelings of happiness.

Money struggles *can* affect your level of happiness. You should have your life put together in a way that even this does not hurt your happiness, but for most people, money challenges are very stressful. Making money will not make you happy, but it can certainly reduce this kind of stress.

Take a moment and do the following exercise: List your top five problems. Write them down. Now look over the list and ask yourself how many of these problems could be solved if you had money in abundance. If having more money makes them go away, the problem itself isn't really the problem—*a lack of money* is. This demonstrates how money can eliminate some problems.

Moreover, without financial freedom, you are not truly free. Many people don't have the influence they could have because they are bogged down by their finances. Increased resources allow you to more effectively pursue your life vision.

> **Many people don't have the influence they could have because they are bogged down by their finances. Increased resources allow you to more effectively pursue your life vision.**

Even wealth does not automatically increase happiness, but applying true principles (in all areas of life) does directly help people feel happier. In order to be happy, people must *give* happy. As we serve God and others, genuinely seeking to help people be happier, our own happiness increases. This bears repeating: Happiness comes from serving others and getting your life in line with God and true principles, learning who you are and *whose* you are.

The goal is not to become a miser focused on your little pile of money. As we said before, money is a tool, like a hammer. What would you think of a carpenter who fixated on his hammer? It's not cool.

As Chris puts it: "Make money to enable your priorities and service in God's Kingdom." In such service, money is a powerful tool.

Affording It

As you were growing up, did you get tired of hearing the words "We just can't afford it" from your parents? This can be frustrating. But by far, the worst thing would be to have to say the same thing about your life dream.

Sadly, most people are never able to afford their greatest dream, their life vision, their deepest purpose. Real happiness comes from doing what you were born to do, and having the resources to do this is the real purpose of long-term financial fitness. Your goal isn't (or shouldn't be) high net worth, but rather freedom to make choices. Living the principles of financial fitness gives you more options.

Here is the big question everyone needs to answer: What is the result you are going to focus on after you are well on your way to becoming financially fit and don't have to pursue money anymore? What is your life vision?

What is money, really? The truth is that money is a receipt for your service to others, so your greatest service is what will help you obtain wealth.

USING YOUR TIME, MONEY, AND TALENTS TO GENUINELY HELP OTHERS NATURALLY INCREASES YOUR HAPPINESS. SEEKING MONEY FOR MONEY'S SAKE MAY OR MAY NOT INFLUENCE YOUR HAPPINESS, BUT SEEKING MONEY IN ORDER TO FULFILL YOUR STEWARDSHIP AND SERVE AND BLESS OTHERS AUTOMATICALLY INCREASES IT.

Our friend Chris is a young undersheriff in a crime-filled county in Michigan. He is also a successful entrepreneur and has owned several profitable businesses. In addition, he is an accomplished bodybuilder and multiple-time Iron Man finisher.

Public recognition, financial success, and personal achievements, however, were not enough. Chris wanted to give back. Being a police officer, he was in a unique position to see want and need in the inner neighborhoods of his city. Inspired by Jesus's feeding of the 5,000 in the gospels, Chris and some associates decided to arrange for free home-cooked meal distribution in the same neighborhood every Tuesday.

Their goal was nothing more than to fill a need and give something back to their community. For years now, thankful citizens have been lining up to meet Chris and several other smiling faces at the serving line. Chris insists on being there in person himself, rain or shine, each and every week. More than just food, Chris and his associates give love. It is obvious to everyone that someone cares. Chris and people like him everywhere have discovered that giving back is really what it's all about.

Take Action

Take a few moments right now to write out your plans to apply the principle covered in this chapter. List ways you might give more of your time, talents, and resources to help others and make a positive difference in your church, community, nation, and so on.

The Big Seven

Understanding and applying these first seven principles of financial fitness will put anyone on the road to financial success. It is impossible to live these principles without seeing a significant improvement in your finances. In fact, if you stopped right here and didn't read any more of this book, but consistently applied these seven laws of financial fitness, you would see your financial picture improve drastically.

There is an old and poignant saying that goes something like this: "The basics are the basics are the basics." Living them brings success, just as surely as not living them will keep you struggling financially.

The principles covered in the rest of the book are equally important. And if you are already applying the first seven principles, then as you learn and apply the ones yet to come, you will be firmly on the path of financial fitness and eventually prosperity. Indeed, if you are now applying these seven principles, you are already on the way to becoming financially fit.

Successful business leader Claude Hamilton tells the story of how he learned and applied the principles of financial fitness:

When I was a child, money wasn't a subject that was discussed in the home, except for one thing: the scarcity of it! When I left home at the age of sixteen and enrolled in the military, I soon found myself with a steady income, and bankers and credit card companies were more than happy to offer me credit. I didn't know how to budget, balance a checkbook, or save for a rainy day, and I didn't know the benefits of saving and earning compound interest.

I found comfort in my misery because all of my friends were in the same circumstances. I knew there were people who didn't live this way, and I knew the difference was that they knew something I didn't.

I went to the bookstore and quickly found some books with great promises in their titles telling me how to get rich in real estate, buy gold, and play the stock market. I bought them all on credit and went home feeling that I would soon be rich.

Needless to say, those books weren't the solution. When I met a friend named Dave, I noticed that he had a very different attitude about money. When my group of friends bought extra large coffees, he would buy the small size. When we ate out and I bought pop and appetizers and dessert, Dave kept it to a minimum. He didn't drive the newest cars, and he didn't have the flashiest clothes. But I noticed something that set him apart from the others: it seemed he didn't fight about money with his wife.

After watching him for a while, one day I asked him why he was different in the way he used money. Instead of holding court and lecturing me on money, he told me he'd get me a book. Later, he handed me a copy of *The Richest Man in Babylon*. At the very beginning of this book, I learned that I needed to save a portion of all my income. This started my study of the principles of financial fitness. Because I was already familiar with many "get-rich-quick" books, I quickly realized that the book Dave gave me was very different. It taught with principles and took a long-term view. I immediately began to put its concepts into practice and learned a valuable lesson about sources of information. It was good to have a mentor who could differentiate what was good info and what was bad. I began to look for other books that taught real principles of lasting financial wisdom. But it was difficult to find everything I needed, since many books just had one or two principles tucked away between things that didn't really help.

One of my biggest hurdles to overcome was trying to "keep up with the Joneses." Most people want to look rich but end up being poor. I decided that being financially secure was better than looking like I had money. So I started to practice delayed gratification.

Many people get this mixed up. They think not buying something that you can't afford is delayed gratification, but in fact, the key is to not buy everything you can afford. Getting in a habit of saving is the first key. And if you are in debt and can't afford a Hummer, then not buying one isn't delayed gratification; it's just not being stupid! Delayed gratification is when you *can* afford something but you hold off because you prioritize your financial security over a new toy or something you don't need.

Over time, I learned more and more about handling money and making long-term logical decisions instead of short-term emotional decisions. Today, I am excited that I will be able to help my children, family, and friends so that they won't ever have to go through the same pain if they'll simply apply the basic principles of financial fitness.

The basics work, and those who apply them will get financially fit.

Summary of Part I—Basics

- Most people do not apply the principles of financial fitness, and as a result, they constantly struggle with their finances. Our invitation to you is to be the exception, to join the few, the 5% who learn and apply the principles of financial success.
- Here are the basic, foundational principles of financial fitness covered in Part I:

  - PRINCIPLE 1: It's not what you make but what you keep that determines financial success. Pay yourself first and save what you pay yourself.
  - PRINCIPLE 2: Money is a gift. It has a specific use. This means that you have a stewardship. You are to use your money for something that matters, for your family and beyond.
  - PRINCIPLE 3: Live within your means. Always. No exceptions. Period. Follow a good budget. Give each spouse a small allowance so you have a little discretionary money each month, and don't nitpick each other on the little things.
  - PRINCIPLE 4: Stop getting financial advice from broke people; get it only from those whose finances you want to emulate.
  - PRINCIPLE 5: Consistently budget and save for unexpected expenses.
  - PRINCIPLE 6: Pay 10% of your income to tithing. Give even if you are really broke. Giving puts you in a mindset of abundance and puts any financial worries in their proper perspective, so it should not be

limited to just tithing. The Bible categorizes giving as 1) tithes and 2) offerings.

> PRINCIPLE 7: Using your time, money, and talents to genuinely help others naturally increases your happiness. Seeking money for money's sake may or may not influence your happiness, but seeking money in order to fulfill your stewardship and serve and bless others automatically increases it.

- This book is designed not just for information but for *transformation*; each reader should outline in writing how he or she is going to implement these principles in everyday life.
- If you have skipped any of the assignments in this book or failed to write down your plan for each of the seven principles covered so far, stop right now and do these vitally important exercises. They will put you directly on the path of financial fitness.
- Once you are doing all seven of the basics, focus even more deeply and learn to master them. Make each of them a habit, an autopilot part of your life.

PART II

OFFENSE

"MOVE THE CHAINS!"

The goal of offense in the game of football is to score, but most coaches teach that the real goal of every play is to move the chains—because if you keep getting first downs, you will eventually score, but if you focus on scoring, you might not get a first down, and you will end up having to give the ball to the other team. In baseball, the same principle applies to focusing on trying to get on base every time instead of focusing on getting home runs. This is excellent advice for financial fitness: Forget "get-rich-quick" schemes and just follow the proven daily principles of financial success covered in this book. In Part II, we will address the attitudes, values, and skills of increasing your prosperity, one principle at a time.

An ancient Greek belief held that: "God loves the righteous, but He blesses the bold."

A more modern saying illustrates the same point: "There is magic in big dreams!"

SEVEN

Moneyviews

I would rather carry around a plastic bag with five thousand Euro inside, than carry around a Louis Vitton/Gucci/Prada bag with only one hundred Euro inside!
—JOYBELL C.

Most books on personal finance focus on defense only (how to get out of debt, protect your money, and prepare for contingencies). These are all very important. As Luke 16:10 (KJV) emphasizes, "He that is faithful in that which is least is faithful also in much: and he that is unjust in the least is unjust also in much." However, defense alone is a poor plan to free a person from the Financial Matrix. A proper plan for financial fitness must include both defense and offense just a Warren Buffett said: 1) Eliminate debt (defense), and 2) Invest in self-education (offense). In other words, teams (and families) that win must learn to play defense and offense. With playing defense alone, it would typically take twenty years or longer to get out of the Financial Matrix, but by adding an offense, one can accomplish this impressive feat in much less time.

An attitude of abundance is central to financial fitness.

We will cover financial offense (making more money) first and then defense (protecting one's resources) later because the values and attitudes of financial offense are naturally abundant, aggressive, and bold. Successful financial offense requires initiative, innovation, ingenuity, and tenacity—the entrepreneurial values.

Worldviews

One of the most important influences on your spending and borrowing (or not borrowing) habits comes from your basic views on money. These views can be changed—indeed they often *must* be changed if you want to become financially fit—but first you need to understand which view(s) of money you currently hold.

The word *worldview* came into vogue in the 1990s and has been popularized by philosophers and media pundits who debate spiritual and political matters. It refers to the lens through which people see and interpret the world around them.

Where a *view* consists of a person's thoughts and feelings on any given topic, a *worldview* is a general philosophy of life that includes a person's combined perspectives on life, relationships, money, education, career, politics, economics, truth, entertainment, and so on. All information and observations pass through this overarching lens and are colored by each person's worldview.

Similarly, each person also has a *moneyview*, whether he or she consciously realizes it or not. In our nearly two decades of dealing with people and their finances, we have slowly awakened to the fact that how people are doing financially is often a direct result of their moneyview. Just as with worldviews, there are several different moneyviews, and each of them leads to its own ramifications.

Ten Moneyviews

These include the following:

1. Money as a Mystery: In this moneyview, people seem to have no clue how money is made, how it is retained, and how it works. As a result, those with this view tend to think that others who are successful financially are somehow "lucky."

From this viewpoint, following the principles of financial fitness is like gambling—it will work if you are lucky and fail if you're not. People with this moneyview stay financially strapped until they adopt another, more accurate, view and begin applying the principles of financial fitness.

2. Money as a Master: From this perspective a person's entire life is lived in bondage to paying the bills. The focus is on the lack of money, the need for more money, and the drudgery of scraping by. People with this view are consistently telling their children, "We can't afford that... We can't afford this... We just can't afford it, honey." At the same time, they often use consumer debt on a daily basis to purchase things they believe they can't afford—but must have.

   They routinely use phrases such as, "I have to go to work," or "Another day, another dollar." Ask them how they are doing today, and instead of saying, "I'm well, thank you," or "I'm doing great. How about you?" they will reply, "I'm staying busy!" or "I'm keeping the wolf away from the door!"

   As a result, they are always behind in their finances. They buy things before they have the money for them, and they live their lives feeling enslaved to paying off their debts. Their debts really are their masters.

3. Money as a Monster: This worldview occurs when the Money as Master problems last a long time and get increasingly worse. In this condition, financial pressures become so large that they dominate a person's thoughts and affect him or her emotionally. The overwhelming strain of financial struggles negatively influences every part of the person's life.

Often at this stage, relationships are damaged and health is compromised.

4. Money as a Major: A person with this moneyview applies most of his focus and fascination on how to acquire more. Money becomes the only measure of success in his mind and the only goal he really cares about. In this situation, money is an idol. Gaining more money takes over the life of any person with this moneyview.

This viewpoint frequently leads to a series of failed "get-rich-quick" schemes and a reality TV approach to money: "If I can just win a reality TV show or the lottery, I'll be set for life." A lot of money and effort is wasted in such schemes, and those with this moneyview seldom give any credence to the solid, proven principles of financial fitness.

Or, even more alarming, people with this view sometimes compromise their integrity because money is more important to them than their character.

5. Money as a Motivator: This is the condition whereby money is used to push one to higher achievement and greater contribution. This can be motivating for selfless or selfish reasons—usually a combination of both. Beware of this moneyview because it often creates unhealthy approaches to work, relationships, and life.

However, being motivated toward one's higher goal and life purpose, and using money as a tool on the path to this important stewardship, is a healthier and more effective motivation.

6. Money as a Manipulator: In this moneyview, people use their money to get what they want out of other

people. This is where the philosophy of "Money is power" comes from. This is a very dangerous approach to money because it sets the person up to hurt people he considers inferior—and to rationalize dishonest behaviors as, "It's just business." Many who are caught in this rut are also fearful of those they consider their financial superiors.

A person seeking money for power will never achieve his dreams because he will never have enough power (and, therefore, money). This is a path to ruined relationships and loneliness.

7. Money as a Minimizer: This is the condition where the presence of money minimizes one's ambitions. If a minimizer has enough money for now, he gives up on his life goals and stewardship. This moneyview is rampant with complacency and mediocrity.

8. Money as a Maximizer: A person with this view is driven to utilize his or her money to make a greater contribution and maximize his or her potential. This is usually much more selfless and altruistic than #5 above. True maximization helps you live up to your potential while helping others to do the same.

   People with this moneyview discipline themselves to live the principles of financial fitness, make financial decisions based on a long-term vision, adopt the habit of delayed gratification, and use the compounding nature of money to build businesses and achieve their dreams.

   > **Money is a maximizer of your life purpose.**

9. Money as a Monument: In this view, money is used as a status symbol, to build a reputation, or as an

attempt to establish an immortal family legacy. This moneyview is nearly always unhealthy and damaging—to those who apply it and to those close to them.

10. Money as a Menace: Those with this moneyview use money as a destructive force in their own lives and in the lives of others around them. They feed addictions, cause fights, or lose their time and energy to the desperate need to get and spend more money.

Choose Your Moneyview

Part of becoming financially fit consists of wisely choosing the right moneyview. Successful people adopt the Money as a Maximizer view, even if they were raised with other perspectives. As you consider this list of popular moneyviews, it may be helpful to ask yourself the following questions:

- Which moneyview best represents where you are right now?
- Which of these moneyviews have you encountered in the lives of other people in your life?
- Which have you followed for a period of time in your life?

Notice that several of these views are quite negative. What are you doing to make sure you have a positive and productive moneyview?

The Meaning of Money

All of the moneyviews outlined above illustrate the fact that money is always used as a *means*. Therefore, the key question in money matters is: As a means for what? This is why the Bible again and again treats money as a heart issue.

Money in and of itself is not evil, but the heart frequently sees money as a tool for the wrong things. Money becomes a dangerous or productive tool depending on the heart that wields it.

> **Money becomes a dangerous or productive tool depending on the heart that wields it.**

Make sure you choose your moneyview deliberately and intentionally.

PEOPLE WITH THE RIGHT MONEYVIEW DISCIPLINE THEMSELVES TO LIVE THE PRINCIPLES OF FINANCIAL FITNESS, MAKE FINANCIAL DECISIONS BASED ON A LONG-TERM VISION, ADOPT THE HABIT OF DELAYED GRATIFICATION, AND USE THE COMPOUNDING NATURE OF MONEY TO CONSTRUCTIVELY ACHIEVE THEIR DREAMS.

Etch It in Stone!

Think deeply about the moneyview or moneyviews you had as you began reading this book. Write it or them down. Now, write down the view or views you would like to attain. What are you committed to doing in order to make this change? Record this and prepare to make it real.

EIGHT

Invest in Yourself

Libraries will get you through times of no money better than money will get you through times of no libraries.
—ANNE HERBERT

Most people have a lot of baggage where money is concerned. They either love it for its own sake, or they fear it (mainly that they won't have enough of it). Those who master financial fitness do not get caught up in either of these extremes. They see money as a powerful tool.

Think of a master wood artisan. He has many tools, but he is not like a Tim Allen "tool guy" who is really into tools for their own sake. He uses each tool exactly as it was intended, always with his ultimate purpose in mind.

The artisan doesn't love the tools; he loves his purpose. Tools are very important in obtaining that purpose, but they are not the focus. That being said, if you are going to be successful, you have got to love the game. Love the work you do or the purpose you are working toward.

The Power of Vision

Your long-term vision (your dream, your purpose, your stewardship, your life mission) gives you the power to continue your work through whatever setbacks, upsets, and challenges come along.

You already wrote your purpose earlier, and reading it every morning and night will help you keep focused on your real goals. Put your written long-term vision somewhere you can see and read it often. The workbook will help you with this process.

Always keep in mind that your vision, your stewardship and ultimate purpose, is the main reason you need to be financially fit. Few people who are financially out of shape ever really live their dreams, while nearly all who live the principles of financial fitness attain their dreams and achieve their long-term vision.

Investing in you is the best investment you will ever make.

The Best Investment You Will Ever Make

Once you have a written vision and you are living the other basics covered in Part I, it is time to go on offense, to "seize the day," to take powerful action that will move you forward toward your dreams and goals.

A first step in the attitude of abundance is to always remember that your most important investment is an investment in yourself.

A first step in the attitude of abundance is to always remember that your most important investment is an investment in yourself.

In the Industrial Age, people typically had a forty-five-year plan for their job training and career. Most people worked their whole career for one company, and job security was promoted as a top priority. In today's Information Age, this pattern has drastically changed. The instability of companies, jobs, whole career fields, technology, and the economy itself has created a new definition of financial security.

The key is to invest in yourself and to build yourself into the type of person who can always flourish economically. This is the epitome of financial fitness. Your understanding of the principles of financial success, your character in applying them, and your ongoing efforts to improve yourself are powerful investments.

In the twenty-first century, technology is shrinking the power and reach of many big corporations, but it is creating more opportunities for those who have entrepreneurial values (initiative, ingenuity, innovation, and tenacity, among others). In today's economy, the only true and lasting financial security is being the kind of person who can always succeed, regardless of what happens.

Investing in *you* means becoming such a person. One of the most important steps of investing in yourself is obtaining a high-quality education in finances and leadership. We are not talking about formal schooling here, which too often actually gets in the way of a great education, but rather of really understanding and applying the principles of financial fitness and effective leadership.

The value of this kind of education cannot be overstated. It makes all the difference in your ability to find and take advantage of economic opportunities.

Brain Investment

Investing in yourself means getting an excellent education, especially in the fields of family, finances, and leadership. It also means putting yourself on a self-directed educational journey of reading about leadership, financial principles, and other important fields of human knowledge.

The most successful leaders are avid readers, always reading and learning more about old areas of interest and also new topics of importance. Never forget this truism: Leaders are readers.

Invest in your brain. Read books and listen to audios that help you constantly learn more. If you lost everything, you'd still have your brain, your knowledge, and your wisdom.

Ironically, most people who don't have much money and constantly struggle financially will make many wasteful purchases but resist the idea of buying books or audios that teach them about financial success and leadership. They avoid paying for self-improvement but then spend hundreds of dollars on candy, pop, and other sugary treats (not to mention the dental bills that inevitably follow) and various "toys." And sadly, by example, they teach their children to do the same.

Sometimes even people who subscribe to excellent learning and leadership programs think they can save money by cutting them, but this is like cutting out food. The key is to cut things that are *not* investing in you and to get more books and audios that do help you invest in yourself. Buying books and audios that increase your financial and leadership wisdom is not an expense; it is the best investment of all.

> **Whatever you do, don't cut back on brain investment.**

Whatever you do, don't cut back on brain investment.

FINANCIALLY FIT PEOPLE ARE AVID READERS AND CONSISTENTLY INVEST IN THEMSELVES BY INCREASING THEIR FINANCIAL AND LEADERSHIP EDUCATION, SKILLS, EXPERIENCE, KNOWLEDGE, AND ABILITY.

George and Jill Guzzardo worked in the health care profession as a physical therapist and a registered nurse, respectively. Although they made good incomes, the Guzzardos lived paycheck to paycheck, carried a $4,000 balance on their credit cards, and had two car payments that amounted to another $800 per month. Their incomes, in other words, went to service their debt lifestyle.

However, this began to change when the Guzzardos became business owners and began studying the principles of financial fitness. The Guzzardos quickly eliminated all extraneous expenses and applied the savings to invest in their new business. And as they reduced spending in various unnecessary areas of their lives, they increased their investment in financial and leadership learning.

Over the next couple of years, the Guzzardos paid off their credit card balances and car loans, and as their business continued to grow, they were eventually able to quit their day jobs. Moreover, their business provided enough income to pay off their home mortgage in its entirety, allowing the Guzzardos to move into a beautiful hacienda in Arizona, own three cars with no payments, and retain their Michigan residence as well. George and Jill are living proof that hard work and smart work can move mountains, and that learning and applying the principles of financial fitness really works.

More on Investing in You

Investing in you also means engaging in entrepreneurial projects and gaining experience in leadership. If you have a job, it means doing the same thing as an intrapreneur—thinking like an entrepreneur, a leader, and an innovator at your work, rather than just fitting in to your job description.

It means adopting an ownership mentality, thinking and acting like an owner rather than just settling for an employee mentality. Focus on the owner mentality in your choices, work, interaction with others, and in all tasks, character opportunities, and relationships whether or not you are actually the owner—as an entrepreneur or intrapreneur, or both.

Investing in you means creating value for yourself, in whatever you are currently doing. The work you do for your employer is like carrying buckets of water back and forth for money, but the business you build yourself is like a pipeline that keeps bringing you the water even when you stop working.

This idea of the pipeline versus the buckets is important. The work you do for an employer brings you active income (in exchange for your labor and time), while the business you build brings passive income (which continues to pay you even when you aren't working). You may be carrying buckets for your employer, but your focus is on building a pipeline for your long-term vision and dream. We will have more to say on this later, but part of investing in you is beginning to create that pipeline of passive income.

As you truly excel in your current role, you will naturally be given more responsibility, and as you do the same with the new duties, you will build yourself into a better and better leader.

This is why the offense side of finances is so important in achieving financial fitness. Whatever you are working on right now in your life, truly excel at it in order to fully invest in yourself. The natural result will be progress and increasing prosperity and opportunities.

FINANCIALLY FIT PEOPLE EXCEL AT THE WORK AND PROJECTS THEY ARE DOING NOW, AND AT THE SAME TIME, THEY INVEST IN THEMSELVES IN ORDER TO ACHIEVE THEIR LONG-TERM VISION.

The combination of focusing daily on your long-term vision and dream while truly excelling at your current work and projects is extremely powerful. As you master tasks and surpass expectations, you will undoubtedly be given more responsibility, and because you are focused on your long-term vision, the additional duties will inevitably lead you in the direction of your dreams.

Of course, all of the preliminary seven principles of financial fitness directly help you invest in yourself as well. Paying yourself first is an investment in your future, and focusing on your life stewardship makes you a person of substance. Living within your means, taking advice from the right people, and preparing ahead for emergencies are all investments in your character, discipline, and personal strength.

And consistent giving and service invest in you by making you the kind of person who helps improve the world. You want to be this kind of person because your long-term vision and dreams truly matter. And your investment in building your passive income over time will make you a person with resources to match your talents, skills, and life purpose and will enable you to do more good.

The Mindset of a Winner

All of this combines to help you adopt the mindset and habits of a winner. Some of the work of investing in yourself will be helped along by others. Investing in you means finding and really listening to excellent mentors. Few things are as beneficial.

Also, as you swim upstream against the current to build something significant, facing financial ups and downs, making tough decisions, enduring rejection and criticism, and tackling other similar challenges, you will have many opportunities to give up.

One of the best investments in yourself is making the choice to keep working, to not let anything get in the way of your dreams, to keep trying, and to refuse to give up. This is an investment in courage and persistence, both of which are required for real success in any field.

Another key investment in yourself comes from victory over internal struggles, such as the battle between settling for "pretty good" and instead going the extra mile and pushing yourself to greatness. Every person who wants to succeed in any important endeavor faces this challenge, and as you invest in yourself by choosing greatness (instead of settling for mediocrity or even "good" work), you will become the kind of self-reliant leader who can always flourish.

Nearly every successful person also faces such formidable inner struggles as: "But I just don't like that kind of work," and "I'm just not that kind of person." These are actually fallacies because you are capable of coming to like the type of work needed for the success of your dreams, and you can develop the skills and attitudes to be the kind of person who achieves what you want to accomplish.

Investing in yourself means overcoming all such challenges, keeping focused on your dreams, and constantly reading, thinking, learning, excelling, and preparing yourself for increased opportunities and success. As Winston Churchill counseled, never, never, never give up.

Write Your Plan

By now, you already know the drill. Brainstorm and write out your plan to implement Principles 9 and 10. How can you truly excel—at a whole new level—in your current responsibilities? This one thing alone will bring increase.

In addition to studying and applying the material in this book, list ways you can invest in yourself and create a significantly improved you. How can you invest in your leadership education and experience? In your financial wisdom? In your skills, knowledge, and abilities? How can you become an even more avid reader? What mentors do you need? What advice from current mentors do you need to follow more closely?

What other things can you do to truly invest in yourself?

As always, put your ideas and plans in writing. Then choose the best and implement them immediately. Make your best investment (in you) pay huge dividends through your plans and actions in the months ahead. Get started now!

NINE

Make Money Your Servant, Not Your Master

Don't set your goals by what other people deem important.
—FROM *THE PRINCE AND THE PAUPER*

J. Paul Getty was once considered the richest man alive, but at his funeral, the only people who showed up were those who expected money from his will. He was rich, but his life was far from abundant or wealthy. The Bible asks in Mark 8:36 (NKJV), "For what shall it profit a man if he gains the whole world, and loses his own soul?"

From a 30,000-foot view, your financial goals should not be about getting a high net worth but about increasing your worth to God, family, country, and society. This means gaining real mastery over your finances in order to become a master of your vision and dreams.

> **Your prosperity, wealth, and privileges are not ultimately for your pleasure but for your purpose.**

Learn to make money your servant, not your master. This starts with mastering yourself. Never compromise principle, morality, or your responsibilities to family and loved ones in your search for money. In short, never sacrifice principles for possessions.

Indeed, your prosperity, wealth, and privileges are not ultimately for your pleasure but for your purpose. It is essential to keep this in mind.

The modern sayings "It's just business," "Perception is reality," and "Business as usual" frequently mask the reality that profit is sometimes used as an excuse for dishonesty. In truth, if something is wrong, it is wrong, even if "it's just business."

Perception is not reality. Reality is reality, no matter what Madison Avenue claims. And "business as usual" is no excuse for losing your integrity. If something shady is "usual," make sure you take the *unusual* path. It may be the path less traveled, but it is the road to true success.

> **Perception is not reality. Reality is reality.**

Thoreau once suggested that in a truly unjust society, the only just men would be found in prison. Fortunately, our society allows us to influence positive change without such a drastic result, but it is still vitally important to stand up for justice and freedom.

Alexsandr Solzhenitsyn told students at Harvard that as bad as Soviet Communism had been, the Russian people should not follow the American model either. He explained to the shocked audience that one of the biggest problems with modern America is that in much of the business community, the most important question guiding corporate decisions is not, "Is it right?" Instead, he told them, big business too often just asks, "Is it legal?"[9]

Such a trend doesn't bode well for the United States or other advanced nations who follow this sad guideline. But you can help turn this around by standing up for integrity and principle. As mentioned earlier in this book, example is everything in leadership.

NEVER SACRIFICE PRINCIPLES FOR MONEY OR POSSESSIONS. BE HONEST. KEEP YOUR INTEGRITY. KEEP YOUR PRIORITIES IN THE RIGHT ORDER.

You want to be the kind of leader who lives the principles of financial fitness; becomes successful, prosperous, and wealthy; and whose funeral is attended to overflow by people sharing stories of how you helped, mentored, blessed, and inspired them.

Raymond's Story

At one recent funeral, Raymond's sons, daughters, and grandchildren spent hours listening to surprising stories about their father and grandfather—told by people they had never met. They listened to the many tales about money he had donated to various causes and needy people, and they wondered where he had gotten all his money. He had certainly never seemed rich to them, though he had paid for college and many opportunities for a large family.

Still, they had lived like a normal middle-class family, so they wondered at all the donations and investments in business start-ups people told them about. Their father had been a salesman, and they knew he had done well, but the extent of his generosity was astonishing.

But the best part came as they heard of the time he spent a week hiking with the scouts and how his words and example changed one young man's life forever and about the time a lady was stranded on the highway while driving through town, and the only person she could think of who lived in the city was the salesman she had purchased things from over the years.

She called him, and he came at three in the morning in snowy weather to put her and her children in a hotel, tow the broken car, and return it the next day all fixed up. He would not hear of being paid back for the hotel or the repairs.

As the family heard dozens of similar accounts over the course of the day, they marveled at the man they were burying. They knew he had been a loving and attentive father, but they had no idea what a great purpose his life had fulfilled.

When they learned, one by one, of the many young men and women their father had put through college, of the uninsured home he had rebuilt anonymously after a fire (without telling anyone but his wife), and of the family whose husband and father was in prison that, amazingly, got a check each month in the mail that covered all of their needs, they were moved to tears.

Compare this to the story of J. Paul Getty's funeral above. Certainly, true financial fitness means attaining wealth and abundance in order to live your purpose and bless others rather than just to gain money and possessions.

When Raymond's will was later read to the family, the amazement grew as many riches were thoughtfully distributed. "Who knew?" the family wondered.

The principles of financial fitness are real, and they work. Learning and applying them will enable you to live your purpose and be a blessing to many.

Three Essential Values

There are at least three key values of financial offense. The first is to **maintain your autonomy** (freedom to choose your way) both personally and as a society. If you do not have the freedom to weigh your options and determine your own direction, you will be limited in your ability to increase your financial fitness.

One of the most obvious ways you can lose autonomy is through debt. Another is by allowing your nation to take away the freedoms of its citizens. Yet another is to ignore the principles of financial success, like failing to pay yourself first and save large amounts of money over time.

A second important value is to **stick to your purpose.** This means clearly knowing your goals and dreams, avoiding distractions, and making sure you do what matters. Stephen Covey taught that while management (doing things right) is important, leadership (doing the right things, specifically the things that bring about your purpose) is even more important.

The third value is to **achieve mastery** and become excellent at what you do. In financial fitness, this means being superior at applying the laws of finance outlined here and becoming excellent at your work. For example, if you have to work sixteen hours a day to support your family, you are either working too much or you haven't yet mastered your work. It usually takes about 10,000 hours to gain mastery, so be willing to work very hard at first to gain mastery. Most people don't follow this path, but rather put in around 5,000 hours trying to achieve mastery of one thing before switching to another focus for 2,000 or 3,000 hours.[10]

The better path is to put in the time to gain mastery of one thing and then build on it as you develop a pipeline-type income that will fund your purpose, vision, and dream.

If you decide to master something else later, put in the 10,000 hours and then take the time to apply what you have learned. In such cases, combine your multiple masteries to bring your unique influence to the world—always with an eye toward your stewardship and vision.

DO THE WORK TO GAIN MASTERY IN WHAT YOU DO (USUALLY ABOUT 10,000 HOURS).

This is the ultimate level of investing in yourself, and it is the natural path to financial fitness.

Success is not as easy as winners make it look because once they have put in the 10,000 hours, it might not seem like they are doing all that much for the return they are getting. But it is also not as hard as losers make it seem because they either do nothing or give up after doing 2,000 to 5,000 hours of intense work instead of enduring until they have achieved mastery.

> **Success is not as easy as winners make it look, but it is also not as hard as losers make it seem.**

As business leader Tim Marks puts it, "Wherever you go, there you are." His wisdom is exactly right! You are your level of financial fitness, just as you are your level of physical fitness. Living the principles of financial success in this book will help you increase your level of financial fitness.

Take Action

Create a written plan to implement the principles covered in this chapter. List your priorities and commitments and remind yourself that you will never compromise them. Your learning is only as good as the real, lasting changes that you put into effect. Make money your servant and put in the time to gain mastery over what you do.

TEN

The Power of Multipliers

No snowflake in an avalanche ever feels responsible.
—VOLTAIRE

By now, you have gotten the feel of how this works. This book contains the principles of financial fitness, taught by mentors who have applied these principles themselves, attained prosperity and wealth, and greatly lived their dreams.

Each time you learn a new principle, you apply it to your life and stewardship and plan (in writing) how to effectively put it into action. Then you do it.

This is the pattern of financial fitness, and if you have applied the principles outlined so far in this book, you are getting in financial shape and starting to see a realistic road to truly living your dreams. In fact, if you pay close attention, you will see that you have begun reversing bad financial momentum in your life and started building momentum toward a flourishing financial future.

This is because finances are like snowflakes. One of them will hardly cause a flood or influence the world in any significant way. Indeed, one snowflake doesn't matter much at all. But enough snowflakes can create an avalanche.

Likewise, one bad financial choice might not break you, but it will start a pattern that could. And one good financial choice naturally leads to another and then another. There is massive energy and power in momentum, so learn to shift and keep your financial momentum going in the right direction by applying each principle in this book.

The Power of Compounding

Albert Einstein said that compound interest is the eighth wonder of the world. Those who understand it, collect it, while those who don't, pay it (as the old saying assures us).

Compounding is profound in other ways beyond paying interest. Using multipliers to build your wealth is the focus of financial offense, while removing multipliers from your expenses and debts is the key to defensive financial techniques.

Ask yourself: Are you a multiplier for yourself, or are you multiplying somebody else's wealth (your bank and credit card companies, for example)? Do you have interest working for you or against you? Did you wake up this morning more broke than you were yesterday, or closer to wealth?

> **Albert Einstein said that compound interest is the eighth wonder of the world.**

These are not hard questions to answer. You either have the money for a purchase, or you don't. You are either pregnant, or you aren't. You are either heading in the right financial direction, or you are heading in the wrong one.

> **Do you have interest working for you or against you?**

We will have more to say about paying interest later, but for now, let's focus on what you are multiplying in your life.

First, are you stuck in the habit of saying "Yes" to potential purchases? Most people are. The first question they ask is, "Can we afford it?"

Financially fit people, in contrast, ask different questions. They first ask, "Do we *really* want this? Will it help our purpose and dream? *How* will it help our purpose and dream? In what ways might it be a distraction? Will it cost more money to take care of it or keep it (through things like insurance or annual fees)?"

Even if they answer "Yes" to all these questions, they still follow up and ask, "Would saving or investing the same amount be a bigger help to our purpose and vision? Is *now* the best time for this purchase, or would it be less expensive or just better for our family or business at a later date?"

FINANCIALLY FIT PEOPLE DON'T ASK "CAN WE AFFORD IT?" AS MUCH AS THEY ASK "DO WE *REALLY* WANT THIS? WILL IT HELP OUR PURPOSE AND DREAM? *HOW* WILL IT HELP OUR PURPOSE AND DREAM? IN WHAT WAYS MIGHT IT BE A DISTRACTION? WILL IT COST MORE MONEY TO TAKE CARE OF IT OR KEEP IT (THROUGH THINGS LIKE INSURANCE OR ANNUAL FEES)? WOULD SAVING OR INVESTING THE SAME AMOUNT BE A BIGGER HELP TO OUR PURPOSE AND VISION? IS *NOW* THE BEST TIME FOR THIS PURCHASE, OR WOULD IT BE LESS EXPENSIVE OR JUST BETTER FOR OUR FAMILY OR BUSINESS AT A LATER DATE?" THEY CULTIVATE A HABIT OF SAYING "NO" TO PURCHASES EVEN WHEN THEY CAN EASILY AFFORD THEM AND OF PUTTING MUCH OF THEIR MONEY INTO SAVINGS OR INVESTMENTS INSTEAD.

Two Kinds of Multipliers

Note that the people who usually ask these questions can easily afford the purchase. Indeed, there are two kinds of huge multipliers in financial choices: 1) The Spending Multiplier and 2) The Investment Multiplier. People who have been raised with the spending viewpoint have learned the following pattern:

- See something they want.
- Ask if they can afford it.

- If not, decide whether to use debt to buy it OR to save for it and buy it later.
- If they can afford it, decide to buy it.
  (Note that all three choices are about buying it.)

This is the Spending Multiplier, and those who have this habit are usually prisoners of financial struggles because each purchase multiplies the likelihood of repeating the pattern.

The Investment Multiplier follows a different blueprint. These people:

- See something they want.
- Ask if saving or investing the money, instead of buying the thing, would help their long-term goals more than owning the item.
- If the answer is "Yes," they say "No" to the purchase even though they can afford it (or even easily afford it).
- If the answer is that the thing would help their long-term goals better than not buying it, they sleep on it for twenty-four hours or more. They also do their homework: Can they find it at a lower price at a different store or during an upcoming sale? Can they get a discount by building a relationship with the owner or distributor? Can they find something else that is even better? Can they meet the need they are trying to fill in a better way—whether it is more or less expensive?

Both of these multipliers create habits and financial momentum, especially over time, and usually these habits are passed down from parents to children and beyond.

The Spending Multiplier leads to increased financial struggles as people act hastily and make decisions based on feelings of scarcity and anxiety. In contrast, those who use the Investment

Multiplier believe that haste makes waste, focus on spending for real quality and value, end up with stuff that is worth a lot more than what the "spenders" tend to own, and build real wealth.

In fact, those who routinely use the Investment Multiplier end up owning a lot of assets—things that actually bring them more income—while those addicted to the Spending Multiplier end up with a lot of worn out, used up, and broken "stuff" in their garage.

> "If we're not sure, the answer is 'No.'…If we're sure, let's wait and see."
> —Orrin Woodward

When Orrin and his wife Laurie decided to buy their dream home, they knew how important it was to use the Investment Multiplier approach. As they looked at many possible homes and properties, Orrin kept repeating key phrases like:

"The enemy of great is good, so we don't want a good home; we want the truly great home."

"There's waste in haste. Let's go slow, find the perfect thing, and settle for nothing less than our dream home."

"If we're not sure, then the answer is 'No.' Let's wait until we're absolutely sure."

"If we're sure, let's wait and see. Let's make sure something even better doesn't come along."

> "There's waste in haste."
> —Orrin Woodward

When they finally made the purchase, they were absolutely certain that it was the perfect choice.

A Habit of Wisdom

Like snowflakes, financial choices multiply into habits, and habits determine destiny because they run on autopilot in everyday life. They create tremendous momentum.

Thus, one of the most important investments in yourself is to carefully analyze and wisely choose your habits. Reject the habits that don't serve you well, and cultivate habits that are in keeping with your life purpose and bring you what you really want.

Take the time to write out all of your habits. Brainstorm and try to be thorough. Cross off the habits you want to break and circle the habits you want to increase or strengthen.

> **Reject the habits that don't serve you well, and cultivate habits that are in keeping with your life purpose and bring you what you really want.**

Then make a plan for how to change your habits accordingly. This has direct impact on your financial fitness and applies to your whole life as well.

Especially pay attention to whether you are in the habit of multiplying spending or of multiplying investments and other wise assets. Create a habit of wisdom to go along with your other best habits.

Make it a habit to say "No" to potential purchases even when you can easily afford them. Build the habit of weighing each possible expense using the questions of the Investment Multiplier.

This doesn't mean you can't have fun. The key, as you become more financially fit, is to add a "Fun" or even "Spontaneous" line to your budget. Frugally give yourself a bit of money to spend just for enjoyment or on a lark, but keep it within the bounds of your budget. And hold any major purchases to the 24 Hour Rule discussed earlier.

FINANCIALLY FIT PEOPLE ANALYZE THEIR HABITS—IN LIFE AS WELL AS FINANCES—AND WORK TO BREAK BAD HABITS AND CULTIVATE GOOD ONES. THEY THINK ABOUT AND CHOOSE THE HABITS THEY WANT AND NEED TO ACHIEVE THEIR LIFE DREAMS.

If You Aren't Sure, the Answer Is "No"

Another important principle of financial fitness is to create the habit of delayed gratification. Salesmen are taught that people make decisions emotionally and then rationalize them using logic. What we should really do is the opposite! Learn to make decisions after truly thinking them through, and then enjoy your good decisions emotionally later. Practice delayed gratification.

General Robert E. Lee taught one of the most important principles of financial and life success when he told his officer to teach a young soldier to deny himself. Teach yourself the importance of saying "No."

Launching a Financial Revolution in Your Personal Finances

In *The Sun Also Rises*, Ernest Hemingway wrote: "How did you go bankrupt?" The answer is profound: "Gradually, then suddenly."

This applies to so many things in life, especially our finances. The accumulation of snowflakes can clearly pile up a lot of snow, but until the avalanche starts, nobody quite notices how much snow has amassed. The proverbial "straw that breaks the camel's back" is small and light and would usually go unnoticed, but the break comes because people got used to seeing more and more straw being piled up and did not realize just how heavy it had become.

The time to focus on your financial fitness is now, not after more snow (or straw) has accumulated.

Sit down and write out your plan to apply the principles from this chapter in your life. Then carry it out and stick to it! It is your time to become financially fit. Make it happen starting right now.

ELEVEN

Two Great Financial Keys: Spending Habits and Passive Income

There's no such thing as free kittens.
—Brian P. Cleary

In the bestselling book *The Millionaire Next Door,* Thomas Stanley and William Danko researched financial and economic trends and statistics in modern America and found a number of interesting patterns.

Spousal Spending Habits

They discovered that the number one influence on whether or not a couple becomes millionaires is the spending habits of the wife. While this may seem to fly in the face of modern feminism, the statistics nevertheless forced this conclusion. Of course, bad spending habits can be a problem for either or both partners.

Chris once watched a couple carefully budget, plan out their finances, and sit together for hours meticulously clipping coupons to save money. Then the husband came home one night with a big, new, fun purchase. Saving a few dollars on food doesn't help much if you decide you need a new widescreen TV and all the attachments this week!

Imagine how deflating this development must have been for the wife. How likely is she to keep pinching pennies on the true needs of the family?

So certainly spontaneous purchases can wreak havoc on a budget no matter the person's gender. But the research of Stanley and Danko was explicit: in the predominance of cases, the spending habits of the wife were the key indicator of future wealth (or lack thereof).

> **The number one influence on whether or not a couple becomes millionaires is the spending habits of the wife.**

Of course, good spending habits, on the part of *all parties*, are essential to financial fitness. Every person who wants to become financially fit needs to turn the principles of financial success into habits and make them an autopilot part of his or her life.

Active vs. Passive Income

In addition to wise spending habits, another great key to financial fitness is *passive income*. Researchers Stanley and Danko found that most millionaires are seen as just normal people by their neighbors, and they build their wealth slowly through business ownership rather than fancy jobs.

People who start a business, even on the side, and build it up over time are much more likely to become wealthy than others. You can apply all the other principles in this book and obtain wealth over time, but those who apply them in their own businesses to develop a stream of passive income can become wealthy much more quickly.

OWN A BUSINESS, EVEN IF YOU START OUT WORKING ON IT PART-TIME. YOU CAN APPLY ALL THE OTHER PRINCIPLES IN THIS BOOK AND OBTAIN WEALTH OVER TIME, BUT THOSE WHO APPLY THEM IN THEIR OWN BUSINESSES CAN BECOME WEALTHY MUCH MORE QUICKLY.

In our modern society, youth are typically taught to do well in school, go to college or get equivalent career training, and then get the best job they can. The majority of people today follow this path.

But jobs, by definition, provide active income in return for labor, and active income is not as good as passive income. Robert Kiyosaki taught in his book *The CASHFLOW Quadrant* that there are four main ways to make money: 1) to be paid directly as an employee, 2) to be self-employed or a small business owner and get paid for your services, 3) to own a business system and be paid from its profits, or 4) to invest in businesses and be paid for the use of your money.

He pointed out that the truly wealthy in society are nearly always business owners or investors (#3 and #4 listed above) and that the idea of jobs bringing lasting financial success is mostly a myth. Of course, if you need money and are not making it from any of these four sources, getting a job is a better option than simply starving or becoming dependent on the government.

But prosperity is more likely for those who are investors, business system owners, self-employed, and/or small business owners than for those who hold most of the jobs in the world. This is especially true for those who want to develop an unlimited upside in their income.

Moreover, even those who are self-employed or small business owners must go to work in order to get paid, while successful business system owners and investors get paid even if they don't go to work. Passive, or pipeline-type, income funds you regardless of what you do during the day. In contrast, active, or bucket carrying, income only pays you for your labor.

One of the key principles of financial fitness is to increase your passive income, even if you continue to work at a primary active income source.

**INCREASE YOUR PASSIVE INCOME TO THE POINT THAT
1) MOST OF YOUR INCOME IS PASSIVE AND 2) YOU
CAN LIVE OFF YOUR PASSIVE INCOME.**

Of course, if you are currently employed, don't quit your job until your passive income has surpassed your active income (and you have sought professional advice, gotten out of debt, done the proper planning, and so forth). As we said earlier, you can keep carrying buckets for your employer, but it is also helpful to begin building your own pipeline of passive income.

Business Ownership and Taxes

Another major advantage of owning a business is that the government, in an effort to create economic growth, allows business owners to deduct expenses before paying any taxes, while it taxes employees on every dollar earned. This business tax plan is available whether you run a business full-time, part-time, or even just in your spare time from your home, as long as you run it with an honest "expectation of profit," which means you are really trying to make money. Because of the dramatic impact that utilizing the business tax code has on your finances, a very successful attorney that used to represent the U.S. Internal Revenue Service has been quoted as saying, "You would have to be brain dead not to own a business."

In the United States, there is a day called Taxpayer Freedom Day, which is the day that the average person has to work until, in order to earn enough to cover their federal, state, social security, and medicare taxes for the year. As of 2013, that day is April 19 for someone in the median income range. Those who earn higher incomes have to work even longer before they get to keep the fruits of their labor. In addition, most Americans pay 30%-40% of their income just to service their debts. So the average person is paying a minimum of 58%–70% of their gross income in taxes and debt. No wonder we can't seem to ever get ahead!

If you were offered a choice between receiving a $17,000 raise in your annual income from your job or a $10,000 tax savings every year, which would be more valuable? The answer is the tax savings because after paying federal, state, social security, and medicare taxes on your raise, you would be left with an increase of less than $10,000.

Here is another powerful example of the value of finding every legal tax reduction available to you. If you start with one dollar and your money doubles every year, how long would it take you to become a millionaire? The answer is twenty years. But what happens to this same scenario if you have to pay income taxes? Let's assume that you have to pay "just" 35%, which is a fairly reasonable estimate when you add federal, state (provincial in Canada), sales, capital gains, and excise taxes. In the same twenty years, as your dollars double and you pay a 35% tax on the increase, the total amount will only grow to $27,370.

Year	Tax-Free	With Taxes (35%)
1	$2	$1.65
5	$32	$12.23
10	$1,024	$149.57
15	$32,768	$1,829.19
20	$1,048,576	$27,370

Let's look at an example that demonstrates the difference between creating additional income from a business versus what most couples do when they are struggling with their finances. John and Sally are married with two children. John earns $40,000 per year. With this salary alone, they were struggling each month simply to pay their bills, so Sally went out and got a job making $20,000 per year. With this 50% increase in their household income, they couldn't understand why they still seemed to struggle just as much as they did before. Follow along and see why getting that job was not very helpful.

Based on 2013 tax rates, Sally's job created new federal and state income taxes of $4,845 and social security taxes in the amount of $1,530. She drove ten miles per day round trip, five days per week, fifty weeks per year, totaling $1,430 in commuting expenses (valued by the IRS at $.55 per mile). She spent an average of $7 per day, five days per week, fifty weeks per year on lunches totaling $1,750. She had to buy some business clothes, which needed to be dry cleaned, so that cost another $1,200 for the year. And since both John and Sally were working, neither of them wanted to make dinner when they got home, so they started eating out more often, adding $2,000 to their food bill for the year. They needed childcare, which cost $125 per week and totaled $6,200 for the fifty weeks out of the year that Sally worked. After all of these expenditures, the couple was left with only $985 of additional income for the year! Had John and Sally taken the amount they spent on the expenses for Sally's job and invested it into a business rather than a job, most, if not all, of what they spent could have been deducted as business expenses on their taxes, which would have dramatically increased the amount of money they would have gotten to keep.

Of course, we don't think anyone should start a business for the sole purpose of getting tax breaks, but most employees do not realize what tax benefits there are to owning a business. Study up on this as you research your possible business options.

Earn Your Way Free

The goal is to earn your way out of having to carry buckets and work for active income by building a pipeline of passive income and growing it over time. The first step is to reach a point where you have enough passive income that one spouse can stay home and then enough so that both can stay home and focus on building the pipeline.

This is called "earning your way out" of what Kiyosaki calls the "Rat Race." Working for others can be a rat race for many people. It can be a struggle to feel like you are living paycheck to paycheck. But you can change this simply by applying the principles of financial fitness covered in this book, starting with the basics.

If nothing else, increasing your passive income can be a great add-on to your paycheck. If you feel called to do the jobs you are already doing, or other career paths, gaining some passive income on the side can still be very beneficial and provide invaluable experience and the security of an additional income stream.

If you have no idea at this point how to begin building passive income, don't worry. We are going to cover that later in this book. Just know that acquiring passive income should be on your radar screen as a key strategy for building financial fitness and eventually wealth.

Retirement

On the topic of earning things, retirement should not be an issue of age but rather a function of passive income. Too many people define retirement incorrectly. You want to save and invest in order to retire from things that aren't part of your purpose, not from productive work.

> **RETIREMENT SHOULD NOT BE AN ISSUE OF AGE BUT RATHER A FUNCTION OF HAVING ENOUGH PASSIVE INCOME TO LIVE ON FOR LIFE. RETIREMENT MEANS RETIRING FROM THINGS THAT ARE NOT PART OF YOUR PURPOSE SO YOU CAN FOCUS YOUR PRODUCTIVE WORK ON YOUR LIFE MISSION.**

When you have enough passive income to live on for life, you can retire and focus on your bigger purpose. This takes "retirement planning" to a whole new level.

Exercise

Write down the difference between *active* and *passive* income in your own words. Next, write down all of your sources of income and classify each. Do you need to find a passive income to pursue, grow your current one, or both?

TWELVE

Stop Chasing Money and Chase Your Purpose

What would you do if you weren't afraid?
When you finally give wings to that answer then you
have found your life's purpose.
—SHANNON ALDER

How many days could you live your current lifestyle if you stopped working? Take a few minutes, look over your spending records, and figure this out.

Whatever the answer, this is the measure of how financially fit you are at the moment.

Now, figure out how long it will take you to be able to afford to fully live your dream at existing levels of income and expenses. Knowing this is very important, so take the time right now to figure this out. First, write down the top five things that are needed to live your dream. Then, figure out and write down about how much each of these will cost. Next, look at how much you are saving each year and calculate how many years at that rate of savings will be needed to have enough for the top five things in your life dream. This tells you how likely your dreams are without making any changes to the way you are doing things.

For many people, paying for their dreams at current savings levels will take the rest of their life, and some people will never make it unless something changes. Analyzing your dreams, costs, and existing savings can be downright demoralizing for most people. This is because many people are chasing money and hoping—against all evidence—that somehow their dreams will just materialize. But like the fictional $10 million inherited from a relative discussed earlier, this is too often not the case. But don't let this discourage you. Just acknowledge that you want to live your dreams, that there will be a cost involved, and that you need to increase your financial fitness in order to get where you want to be.

We didn't ask you to do this exercise so you will feel overwhelmed or discouraged; in fact, we want exactly the opposite. But being honest about where you are financially is an important step toward becoming financially fit.

We want you to have a good estimate of what your dream will cost and a clear picture of where you are right now. With these two things in front of you, you can identify what kinds of adjustments you really need. Do you need a $10,000-per-year kind of change, or more like a $100,000-per-year sort of change?

Perhaps your dream demands a million-dollar-per-year change.

Mind Your Own Business

Maybe this exercise makes you feel like you will never live your dreams. Or maybe, if you've been applying the principles of financial fitness and doing the assignments over time as you have been reading this book, you may realize that you are closer than you thought. Either way, outlining the price of your dream and comparing it to your current finances will probably lead you to two important conclusions:

1. The path to your dreams is through building your business (entrepreneurship) or taking a true ownership perspective in your job (intrapreneurship).

2. The sooner you get enthusiastically "fired up" and truly build your pipeline of success, the sooner you can live your dreams.

In this chapter, we are talking about wealth—not the kind that means you can sit back, relax, and never work again (though this may be possible when you attain your goals) but rather the kind that helps you live your stewardship and life mission. This kind of wealth seldom comes from a job; it is nearly always the result of building your own business.

Three Keys to Wealth

Robert Kiyosaki says there are three keys to wealth: 1) long-term vision, 2) delayed gratification, and 3) the power of compounding. We have already discussed all of these, but we need to spend more time on them because they are so important.

As you have read to this point, you've probably noticed that we tend to tie every principle in some way to your life vision, mission, stewardship, or dream. That's because the first key to wealth is in making everything work for your life purpose.

You already wrote out your life vision earlier, and every plan you make (after learning each new principle of financial fitness) should somehow be connected to this ultimate goal. Every financial decision you make should point you in the direction of your dream.

> **The first key to wealth is in making everything work for your life purpose.**

For example, if your long-term vision is not clear and you get a financial windfall of some kind, say $5,000, it will be gone very quickly, and you will have little to show for it—because you will be tempted to follow the Spending Multiplier rather than the Investment Multiplier. A fool and his money are soon parted, as Benjamin Franklin predicted. In truth, 93% of people who win the lottery lose it all very quickly.

On the other hand, if you have a clear life vision and financial plan, you will think about the best ways to build your pipeline and move toward your dream, and the $5,000 will enable you to take a significant leap forward.

At the very least, if you're following the principles of financial fitness, you will have an extra $500 on hand—by automatically putting 10% of the $5,000 in your savings when you pay yourself. And the additional money will provide real progress toward your life purpose.

Building Momentum

As you face financial ups and downs, it's okay to feel defeated at times. It's just not okay to stay that way. By clearly identifying and writing down your stewardship, reading it morning and night and keeping it always present in your mind, and making smaller financial decisions and plans with your dream in mind, you've already built important habits that will help you succeed.

> It's okay to feel defeated at times. It's just not okay to stay that way.

Here are a few more suggestions on how to increase your momentum toward your vision.

First, as Stephen Covey taught in *The 7 Habits of Highly Effective People*, begin with the end in mind. How much money do you need to be free (meaning that your passive income is enough to live on and you can work full-time on building your business and fulfilling your purpose)? You need to know this number.

Second, do not fall into the trap of just wanting as much money as possible. You don't want to spend your whole life just working for money. You want to put great effort into attaining your dream, and you want to have the necessary resources to effectively realize your vision.

Third, stay hungry and focus on learning, especially learning to apply the principles of financial fitness.

Fourth, build your business around your mastery and increase your mastery of your business. Too many people make the mistake of gaining mastery in one area and then assuming that it will apply to other things. So they put money into things they don't understand and lose it.

For example, Mark Twain gained great mastery in writing but put his money into things where he had little mastery and went broke. He had to travel and keep writing just to pay the bills. Michael Jordan wasn't all that spectacular at baseball, even though he may have been the greatest basketball player ever. And Isaac Newton invested heavily in what turned out to be the famous South Seas bubble.

In short, even the most brilliant of us are often idiots when we leave our area of expertise, and we would nearly always be better off financially if we remained within our area of expertise and used everything we had to increase our mastery and feed the golden goose!

> **Even the most brilliant of us are often idiots when we leave our area of expertise, and we would nearly always be better off financially if we remained within our area of expertise and used everything we had to increase our mastery and feed the golden goose!**

Put your time and money into what you know, and your mastery and influence will continually increase.

Fifth, choose focus over diversity in your business and finances. Be really good at one thing, not mediocre at many things. Andrew Carnegie taught that good investors put their eggs in one basket and closely watch that basket to ensure its success. (As a matter of fact, he gave this now famous advice to none other than Mark Twain!)

Likewise, Warren Buffett's investment success came from investing in less than twenty companies over four decades and carefully helping each of them obtain real success.[11] He only invested in places where he had a direct say in the choices of the company. In fact, 99% of his net worth is in one stock (in the company he owns).[12]

The reason most people fail is broken focus. To really attain financial success, focus on these things:

1. Truly excel in your current job and projects, as discussed earlier, and simultaneously start a business.

2. Put in the 10,000 or so hours needed to gain mastery over your business while still excelling at your current job.

3. Make a plan to become financially free by reaching a point where your business more than covers your family's needs.

4. Once you are financially free, put your full-time focus on building your business to the point that it funds your life purpose.

We have covered all of these already, but they bear repeating. The key is to focus. Each of these requires deep focus, one at a time. Once you have accomplished one of them, go to the next and give it the same level of focus.

For example, Bill Lewis was a single man building a business in his spare time outside of his job as an engineer in the auto industry. He worked diligently for years growing the income from his business and paying off his debts. Finally, he got to the point where he was out of debt, had accumulated a nice nest egg of savings, and had a passive income larger than his active engineering income.

One day when he spoke with his mentors and ran his business numbers again, Bill was elated to learn that his engineering job had become optional. He was making enough money from his business that he could retire from his job. He commented:

> You can hardly believe it when it really comes down to it. You work and apply the principles you have learned, and it goes slowly at first. Then, all of a sudden it seems, the day arrives and you march in to work to tell your boss you are leaving. I know that's not the desire of everyone, but for me it was a burning dream. You see, I hated my job....
>
> It wasn't really the outside income that did it as much as the financial education I'd gotten that allowed me to get out of debt, accumulate some real savings, and spring myself free to pursue my business full-time. I believe anyone can learn from these principles and do similar things.

Imagine how you will feel the day you reach your biggest goal.

Put It into Action

Identify which of these four is your current needed focus and develop a strategy to make it happen. Add it (in writing) to your previous plans and update them so you have a detailed outline of what to concentrate on as you accomplish the next item on the list. Put your plan into action.

TO REALLY ATTAIN FINANCIAL SUCCESS, FOCUS ON THESE THINGS: 1) TRULY EXCEL IN YOUR CURRENT JOB AND PROJECTS AND SIMULTANEOUSLY START A BUSINESS, 2) PUT IN THE 10,000 OR SO HOURS NEEDED TO GAIN MASTERY OVER YOUR BUSINESS WHILE STILL EXCELLING AT YOUR CURRENT JOB, 3) MAKE A PLAN TO BECOME FINANCIALLY FREE BY REACHING A POINT WHERE THE PASSIVE INCOME FROM YOUR BUSINESS MORE THAN COVERS YOUR FAMILY'S NEEDS, AND 4) ONCE YOU ARE FINANCIALLY FREE, PUT YOUR FULL-TIME FOCUS ON BUILDING YOUR BUSINESS TO THE POINT THAT IT FUNDS YOUR LIFE PURPOSE. EACH OF THESE REQUIRES DEEP FOCUS, ONE AT A TIME. ONCE YOU HAVE ACCOMPLISHED ONE OF THEM, GO TO THE NEXT AND GIVE IT THE SAME LEVEL OF FOCUS.

THIRTEEN

Choosing Your Business

Happy people produce. Bored people consume.
—STEPHEN RICHARDS

We will now address the heart of financial offense. It's time to choose your business. You may already have a business, and if so, you can apply these principles to helping it grow. If you are new to business ownership, you should know the truth right from the beginning:

Less than 10% of new businesses succeed.

This reality does not mean you shouldn't start and build a business; it means that you need to be smart about how you do it. The first key is absolutely vital: Get good mentors! Get advisors who have succeeded in the type of business you are going to build and can effectively help you through the process.

GET GOOD MENTORS AND REALLY LISTEN TO THEM.

Nearly all business failures can be traced to not having good mentors or not following their advice.

What Kind of Business?

To find a good mentor, you need to know what kind of business you will be building. Then you can find mentors who have been successful in the same type of business.

There are two main approaches to starting a business:

1. Building a system
2. Buying a system

Building your own business system requires a great deal of work and can take many years to achieve profitability. One of the best books on building your own business system from scratch is *The E-Myth* by Michael Gerber.

Gerber suggests starting small, holding most of the positions yourself, and hiring people to fill positions only after you have learned each role by personal experience. In this process, he counsels you to do the work of a position, learn the "ins and outs" of what works, and use your personal experience gained from this effort to write a comprehensive description of the job and turn it into an effective, repeatable system.

Then do the same for each additional position in the business. As you complete the system for each role, you can hire employees to fill these positions while you work in and develop systems for other needed jobs. Many start-ups have begun exactly this way.

This process is admittedly slow, and it is one of the reasons that more than 90% of new businesses fail. In fact, many successful new business ventures of the "build it" type are founded by leaders who have built successful businesses of the "buy it" kind first—and later applied their wisdom and experience to building a system from scratch.

Very few people successfully go directly from the world of a job to the demands of a "build it" business system. Many try, and nearly all fail. Part of the challenge is that few "build it" businesses allow people to keep their regular job while they launch a new company.

Buying a System

But many people are able to go from a job to a "buy it" business system and make it successful. They are able to keep their day job while they get their business started, and they can use their employee income to help fund the new venture.

Perhaps the biggest advantage of starting a "buy it" business system is that it comes with much of the work already done—the legal structure, job descriptions, products, leadership training, and many other things that make a "build it" business system overwhelming for most people. Above all, "buy it" businesses sometimes come with mentors who are already succeeding.

There a several kinds of "buy it" business systems. The most numerous are existing businesses that sell you their systems and an ongoing client base and income stream along with their building or rental contract and other fixtures. In some cases, the employees stay as well.

The challenges in such arrangements are numerous because existing businesses also have their share of baggage: contracts that must be fulfilled, perhaps debts, complicated politics between employees and management, etc. It is therefore essential for prospective buyers to put a great deal of work into due diligence before purchasing existing businesses.

Perhaps the biggest difficulty is that people without experience in business ownership seldom do well when they take over an existing organization. They typically come in with the background of an employee, or perhaps just a student, and few companies survive the transition.

Good business system owners usually have a lot of experience as successful leaders, and those with an employee background rarely gain such experience. There are, of course, exceptions—those people who buy a business system despite no ownership experience and who learn through trial, error, and tenacity to make it work.

The other major kinds of "buy it" business systems include: franchises and network-marketing companies. Both typically provide huge benefits in legal groundwork, products, marketing, and leadership training. Both usually have well-established guidelines and systems that are proven effective.

The major difference between the two is that franchises usually require hundreds of thousands of dollars (or more) up front, while network-marketing companies can usually be joined for just hundreds of dollars. Also, network-marketing businesses nearly always have built-in mentors who help the new owners succeed.

Internet marketing expert Eban Pagan said, "Network marketing is a great place to start. You will learn so much if you stick with it a couple of years...because you have to deal with individuals, you have to figure out how another person works. You also get to hang out with successful people. It's one of the fastest paths to get to hang around directly with people who have a success mindset. You can go to conventions, get their information, products, etc. Then all of a sudden it will start to click when you go to talk to people."

Eban points out that network marketing is such a great idea because it gives invaluable experience and learning opportunities for dealing directly with a wide range of people (which is critical to success in any kind of business), and it gets you around top thought leaders and people who are living the principles of success better, easier, and more directly than any other industry does.

Write Down the Pros and Cons

Depending on your background and interests, any of these kinds of business systems might be right for you. As you consider what kind of business system you want to build or buy, ask yourself the following kinds of questions and put your answers in writing.

If you are already a successful business system owner, ask yourself:

- Do you want to start another business system, or grow the one you already own?
- Do you want to build a new business system from scratch?
- Or do you want to buy into a business system opportunity that is already established—so you can focus on growth?
- Have you gained mastery in your current business field?
- Do you want to buy a business system outside your area of mastery and take the time to gain a new mastery?
- Or do you want to buy another business system within your field of mastery?
- Is it time to grow your business system while you continue focusing on your dream?
- Or is it time to sell your business system, or perhaps hire a CEO to run it, and focus more on your dream?
- How can you connect your business to your passions?

If you are not already a successful business system owner, consider the following:

- You probably don't want to buy an existing business system, unless you have a lot of experience in the field, such as from working in a family business. Do you have mastery in this business field?

- Do you have access to the funding to buy the existing company?
- Are you interested in a franchise?
- Do you have access to the resources needed to purchase a franchise?
- Have you looked into networking companies and found one that resonates with your passions and interests?
- Do you want to build a business system from scratch?
- Can you excel more in your current job so you can bring in increased resources to build your business system?
- What are your passions, and how can you build your business system around them?
- Do you have passion for a business system idea but need leadership experience and resources in order to do something about it? If so, do you need a first-tier business system that gives you experience and money for a few years?

> **What are your passions, and how can you build your business around them?**

- In what areas do you want to gain mastery, and are you willing to put in the necessary time in order to do so? And what business system opportunities are available in these arenas?
- Who will mentor you?

Take Action

One of the most important things about building your own business system is to create something that meets and exceeds customer needs by providing real value. When you deliver something customers truly need and that genuinely improves their lives, the value of your business system has the opportunity to grow because it makes a significant difference for the people it serves.

Do your homework. Research and find the right opportunities. They are out there for those who diligently seek them. Find the opportunity that is right for you and then take action.

In summary, good things come to those who start. Even if you make changes to your plan later, by taking action and beginning a business that interests you, you will be far ahead of those who wait around and do nothing.

FOURTEEN

Feed the Golden Goose!

Too many people spend money they don't have...to buy things they don't want...to impress people they don't like.
—WILL ROGERS

We often refer to building a business by saying, "Feed the golden goose!" When your business is paying you, especially in passive income, it truly is like the story of the goose that lays golden eggs.

In essence, there are two uses for your money. One is productive and one is wasteful (and possibly even destructive). Productive spending of money is actually not spending at all, but rather *investing*. Nonproductive spending of money is *consumption*.

The difference between the two lies in what is accomplished by the outgo of your hard-earned money. The key question is: Does the outgo result in a return, or is it gone forever?

At all times, but especially when economic times are tough, spending should be done strategically to minimize the amount that goes to waste, and maximize the amount that goes to something productive. Again, productive means it is building your wealth by being placed into something of value, something that generates cash flow, something that brings back more dollars.

Most people do not think this way naturally, mostly because they were raised with a Spending Mentality and not a Money as a Maxi-

> **Does the expense result in a return, or is it gone forever?**

mizer view. But getting on the road to financial fitness requires adopting a new viewpoint.

A Sad Truth

We are belaboring these seemingly simple points because we have found over the years that financial intelligence and experience is an extreme rarity. It seems few people have ever been taught that money has a purpose beyond its use toward their immediate comfort and gratification. As a result, many people making a six-figure income have spent themselves into oblivion and have nothing to show for it. This reality is incredible, but true.

Difficult financial environments in which the economy slackens, the dollar declines in value, jobs become scarce, salaries go down, overtime pay is retracted, concessions are demanded, and so on only serve to emphasize the point and amplify poor habits.

> It seems few people have ever been taught that money has a purpose beyond its use toward their immediate comfort and gratification.

When these challenging winds blow, the sloppy and financially ignorant (or consumptively addicted) are exposed. Most people are not to blame for the fact that they inherited the wrong attitudes and habits about money, but at some point, we all have to take responsibility and adopt a grown-up view of money.

Most people panic and violently cut back on spending when financial challenges come. The trouble is, they often cut back in the productive areas too. They have wasted so much money and gotten themselves into so much trouble financially that they can no longer (or will no longer) put money into feeding the goose that lays the golden eggs.

As millionaire financial advisor Todd Tresidder stated, "Those with credit card debt and too many bills are more committed to their lifestyle rather than to building wealth."

The financially mature understand that the golden goose must be fed *no matter what*. This means during the good times, when consumptive addiction and wasteful spending are at their most tempting. And it also means during the tough times, when panic sets in and constrictive cutbacks are rushed to like rats fleeing a sinking ship.

> **It is the discipline to use money productively that separates the wealthy from the rest.**

It is the discipline to use money productively that separates the wealthy from the rest.

An Economic Diet

The sad reality is that the majority of people are economically unhealthy and obese and need to go on a diet. No matter how many carnival mirrors the government tries to show us in, most of us are in bad economic shape. The aggregate of private household debt in the United States is now over $3 trillion.

We whine about the government being in debt, from $15–53 trillion (depending on whether you're counting currently funded or future unfunded liability debt), when the U.S. population itself has over $3 trillion in personal debt! The modern credit addiction has really come home to roost, and people are now forced to pay the price.

The housing bubble popped and caused the Great Recession. The game of refinancing your house and taking the equity out and spending it on worthless things is over.

In our economic diet, we need to admit what foods are good to eat and what foods are bad to eat—as applied to finances. Let's elaborate on the difference between consumption and invest-

135

ment because the proper use of money produces more income for you in the future. This is the kind of spending that accumulates assets.

An asset is something that kicks off more income, more cash flow, such as the business we encouraged you to start. A house is not an asset because a house is extremely expensive to own. If you own a house and rent it at a profit, it is an asset. If you live in it, it isn't. This is why we now recommend that some people just rent and let the market go down further (depending on their specific financial situation).

But there is a difference between good spending and bad spending. Consumption is wasted. Investment is designed to bring a later return.

Nonproductive Spending

We are often amazed as we talk with people to hear about the things on which they spend money. Let's go through a list of nonproductive spending. Money, once it is spent, is gone, and usually it is wasted. Remember, this is money spent after people have already paid the heavy tax burden on their income.

Cable/satellite TV, movies (theaters/rentals/purchases/DVD and Blu-ray collections), eating out at restaurants, shopping just for the fun of spending, clothing, fashion, jewelry, magazines, newspapers, music CDs and downloads, foo-foo coffees (the kind that have one-sentence-long names, with the little cup cozy, sipped with your pinky in the air), soft drinks, snacks, sporting events, cigarettes, alcohol, spas, nails, hair and skin treatments, buying the most expensive foods at a grocery store, travel, entertainment of all kinds, hobby equipment, pets, and so on: This is a list of consumption. Most of this is a wasted and reckless spending of money.

None of it feeds the goose that lays the golden eggs. The goose is your business, your income, and your own ability to perform at something profitable, and feeding the goose means putting money into things that bring you back more money than you put in to them.

This is a very simple concept, but few people apply it. Those who do are nearly all financially fit. Those who don't are addicted to financial struggles. It really is this cut and dried.

So why don't more people put a lot more of their money toward feeding the goose? The answer is habit, momentum, and the multiplier effect that occurs when people spend for the wrong things.

Good News

But the great thing about the multiplier effect is that it also creates momentum in the right direction. When people follow the principles of financial fitness outlined in this book, their good choices multiply and create momentum toward prosperity.

The moment of truth, where the rubber really hits the road, is in people's spending choices. We have discussed this from several angles already because it is such a vital principle of money success. In fact, it is the crux of financial fitness: Those who spend productively (feeding the goose so that their spending brings back more money than they spend) get out of debt, become prosperous, and create wealth. And they ultimately use this wealth to accomplish their goals and attain their dreams.

Those who spend more of their money nonproductively on things that bring them no money next month or next year are financially flabby. They never quite grasp the principles of money, and they always struggle to pay their bills—much less live their greatest dreams.

Productive Spending

Productive spending is investment. It means putting money into the YOU, Inc. Investment Hierarchy to build true assets. It is "food for the goose." Think about the story of the goose that laid the golden eggs. Our homes, and their false increase in value that went up for a few years, were not the goose laying the golden eggs. Even though many were led to believe that this was true, it wasn't.

The goose that lays the golden eggs includes your own ability to perform. It is your ability to either do really well in your employment or, even more importantly, to do really well at an entrepreneurial endeavor. Having your own business that helps the economy and generates revenue through productive means—*this* is the goose.

The normal behavior for most people is to be very wasteful and spend money on far too many nonproductive things. (Actually, the first version of this book said, "...spend money on far too many dumb things." Our editor changed it, which we felt was politically correct. But we wanted to say it like it really is, too.) Then they get into trouble financially, and they panic.

You see this in diets, too. People go to extremes and only eat meat, or tomatoes, or simply starve themselves. Extremes are rarely the solution. Extremes rarely work. Going extreme on our bodies does not last very long. Most of us revert back to our old, unhealthy habits and become our old, unhealthy selves.

> **Extremes are rarely the solution. Extremes rarely work.**

Extreme approaches are also destructive because they deprive the body of what it actually needs. Economic diets have the same issues.

Instead of extremes, we need to simply apply the principles of financial success. We need to think, "What is the goose in my life that lays the golden eggs? What can I do at work or in a business that is the most productive? Where can I put energy, time, and money and invest in a way that over time will bring back a return?"

138

What is needed is a wise financial diet that puts a stop to spending money wastefully, such as going out to dinner, buying fancy cars, spending excessively on recreation and entertainment, and other old habits that got you into trouble in the first place. But it isn't enough to stop spending on nonproductive things. You need to put that money into productive uses, things to feed the goose.

Too often people panic and stop all spending. This is good for eliminating the destructive and wasteful consumption, but they need to keep feeding the goose that lays the golden eggs. The principle is this: Feed the goose first. Don't panic and starve the goose.

Make sure the goose is warm, safe, and comfortable. Keep feeding the goose for the long term, so it will become fatter and produce more geese that lay more golden eggs. Don't waste money that should be going to the goose on a consumptive, bad-habit, economically obese lifestyle.

Feeding the Goose

We started with the principle of always paying yourself first. If you remember, we mentioned that the first level of the YOU, Inc. Investment Hierarchy is investing in yourself. You do this by expanding your ability and capacity to create wealth by investing in personal development education and entrepreneurial or intrapreneurial activities and continually funding your savings account on an automatic basis. Your savings is yours to keep and never waste. Always maintain adequate cash savings. But there does come a time when using *some* of your hard-earned savings is more productive invested in building your business rather than sitting in a savings account. Use it wisely, only in ways that will bring in more income than your investment. The concept of investing in your own business is one of the most important principles of financial fitness. Along with your personal capabilities and knowledge, your business is your goose, and by feeding it, you can create a lasting pipeline to wealth and live your dreams.

If you do not feel ready to make this shift yet, then don't. Only take action on this when you have wisely looked at all the pros and cons and know that this is the best place to increase the productivity of your money. And make sure your mentor agrees.

The way to dig yourself out of an economic problem is to figure out what your goose is (or find one) and feed that goose. You might have to sacrifice on the consumption side. You might not be able to do some of the things you wanted to do. Christmas might be a little leaner. But it's not going to hurt you.

> **The way to dig yourself out of an economic problem is to figure out what your goose is (or find one) and feed that goose.**

The Problem Is Widespread

A big, massive, material lifestyle doesn't make you happier. The average American family is in debt and living paycheck to paycheck. Where did we get this idea that it's okay to be in debt and that it's fashionable to sign on the dotted line? Sadly, the answer is often that government promotes this kind of financial flabbiness.

Have you ever seen drug dealers on the corner, hanging out, looking kind of shady? They offer kids a little bit for free first and then provide enticements and incentives for getting more and more and more. Governments often do the same thing.

This is precisely what the U.S. government has done. It has driven interest rates down to almost nothing, given mortgage interest deductions and tax credits to homebuyers, and offered crazy programs like paying people to turn in their old cars.

Now, there's a bright idea! Let's have a whole bunch of people with cars that are paid off turn them in to finance new imports.

Let's encourage all kinds of consumer spending and debt and then call it a good economy.

Clearly, financial fads are not as effective as the simple, solid, proven principles of financial fitness applied over time. Fads fizzle; principles prosper.

For example, years ago lots of people were speculating on real estate and "flipping" houses. Now, the houses are flipping them. Business leader Tim Marks was working as an engineer and decided he wanted to find a way to get out of working so many hours in order to have more time with his family. So he bought into one of those late-night cable infomercials about "no-money-down" real estate and began buying rental properties with a vengeance.

In just one year, he had acquired thirty-three rental homes and, on paper at least, was making the program work. The producers of the real estate product invited him and his family to Florida for a video shoot to promote his "success" and even posted a hypothetical "net worth" on the screen below his photo.

The reality, however, was a bit less glitzy. In a short amount of time, troubles began as tenants destroyed or abandoned properties. Worse, a property manager misappropriated a six-figure amount from Tim over the course of two years, and his cash flow became terribly negative. Struggling to keep the house of cards standing, Tim lived a stressful life of court appearances and frenzied trips to banks.

The whole thing came crashing down and left him in a huge mountain of debt. Tim learned the hard way that "leveraging debt" and using "other people's money" is a lot harder than it sounds. While there may be a big upside for some, Tim found that the downside can be incredibly painful. Instead of finding a way to become financially fit, Tim had become financially reckless, all the while thinking he was doing something responsible for his family and future.

Through a lot of hard work, Tim and his wife Amy learned the principles of financial fitness and dug themselves out of the hole they had created. They eventually built a thriving business and began living the lifestyle they had wanted for a long time.

It is amazing how you'll see all these crazy ads, such as late-night "get-rich-quick" schemes and promotions like, "Protect your investment in your new motorcycle." Investment? A new motorcycle is not an investment. Here is something to remember: If you have to finance your recreation, it isn't time to play.

Again, the habits and momentum of bad financial choices won't make you happy. What makes you happy is being productive and doing the things you were created to do in a vision-directed way, feeding the goose, having victories, growing yourself, and achieving things that matter. These things are much more fun and rewarding than going into debt to buy the next shiny object that catches your eye. As billionaire Steve Jobs once quipped, "Simplicity is the ultimate sophistication."

> **If you have to finance your recreation, it isn't time to play.**

Always remember the principle of feeding the goose that lays the golden eggs. Put your money into food for the goose. Stop wasting money on consumption and start putting money into investments—especially those you control.

USE YOUR MONEY PRODUCTIVELY—BY PUTTING IT WHERE IT WILL BRING YOU BACK MORE THAN YOU PUT IN—RATHER THAN NONPRODUCTIVELY. THE BEST INVESTMENT IS IN YOURSELF AND YOUR OWN BUSINESS. WISELY AND APPROPRIATELY USE SOME OF YOUR SAVINGS TO INCREASE YOUR BUSINESS ASSETS AND RETURNS.

Specifically, the best place to invest is in yourself and in the things that you can do which are productive in the long term. You are your best asset. Invest in you, and invest effectively and wisely in building your business. Don't waste the food for the goose that lays the golden eggs.

> **You are your best asset. Invest in you, and invest effectively and wisely in building your business.**

Carve It in Marble

Update your financial plan to include putting more of your money to productive use, and consider when to use some of your bank account savings in more productive business uses that increase your rate of return.

Warning: Do not take this step until you have built up adequate savings and your business is ready to significantly benefit from the additional assets. Only use this money to fund assets that will bring bigger returns than you put in. Do not use savings to speculate. Only invest this way in your own business, something under your control. Consult your mentor as you make these decisions.

Put these changes in writing, and only take action after discussing them in detail with your top financial mentors.

FIFTEEN

The YOU, Inc. Investment Hierarchy

Money is a great servant, but a bad master.
—FRANCIS BACON

The first principle of financial fitness is to pay yourself first, and by now, you should have been doing this for a while. In this chapter, we'll discuss the seven levels of the YOU, Inc. Investment Hierarchy, which shows the various levels of investments into which your savings will go.

Each level has its own set of guidelines, rules, warnings, and principles of success. The most important thing is to focus on the bottom levels of the hierarchy and only work on higher levels once you have mastered the lower levels. Note that each level as you go up the hierarchy is a less safe investment than the ones below.

Level One: Yourself

Investing in you is the first focus of good investment and the foundational level of the YOU, Inc. Investment Hierarchy. Indeed, investing in you (your education, financial wisdom, leadership abilities, and other skills, knowledge, and strengths) is the most secure kind of investment.

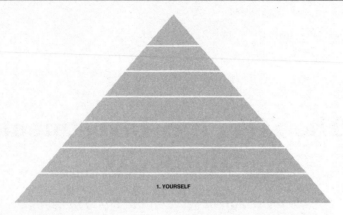

This includes investing in your own business. One of the most

Investing in you is the first focus of good investment.

effective ways to invest in you is to invest in your own business success. Start a business. Build your business. This is a vital process on your path to financial fitness.

Level Two: Emergency Fund

The next level on the YOU, Inc. Investment Hierarchy is your emergency fund, which we have already discussed. In fact, by now, you should have a solid amount saved in this fund. An important milestone of the emergency fund is to put away at least $1,000. This should be done as soon as possible. Sell something or do extra work to acquire this beginning amount *fast*!

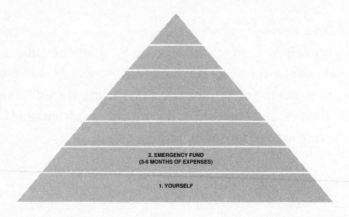

146

Keep saving here until you have at least enough to cover three to six months of living expenses. As your assets and income grow, your emergency fund should increase as well.

Level Three: Survival Preparation

As your emergency fund grows and is well on its way toward covering three to six months of expenses, you can start investing a small portion of your savings into the third level of the hierarchy in order to prepare for worst-case scenarios, such as being impacted by a natural disaster, like an earthquake, hurricane, or tornado; or other events like banks closing, as they did during the Great Depression. Indeed, the generation that survived the Great Depression had excellent investment habits—learned the hard way. It is a good idea to emulate their example.

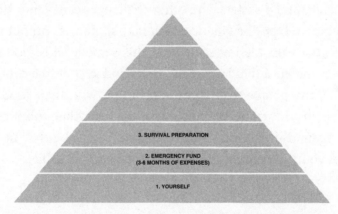

3. SURVIVAL PREPARATION

2. EMERGENCY FUND
(3-6 MONTHS OF EXPENSES)

1. YOURSELF

Saving for a worst case includes the opposite of compounding money, which we will call "impounding." This means putting away various forms of money just in case catastrophic things happen. Stash some cash in a safe, secure, secret place. And in case inflation ruins the value of the currency, put away some silver coins as well. Silver is better than gold for this pur-

> **Saving for a worst case includes the opposite of compounding money, which we will call "impounding."**

pose because in a worst-case world, gold will be very valuable, so a gold coin will be worth a lot more than the food you will want to buy with it.

Small silver coins will be easier to trade for small needs. Gold can be used to effectively protect larger amounts from loss of value due to government inflation (more on this later).

By the way, don't be too extreme about this. We are not doom and gloomers, and we're not predicting a world with roving bandits and no electricity. It could happen, but so could a lot of things. We are simply suggesting that part of sound money planning is to realize that bank holidays and closed banks can happen. They occurred during the Great Depression, even though the world didn't end. But people with some cash and silver were able to purchase food and fuel when others could not. And major storms, natural disasters, and other challenges can come also. So be prepared. Don't be fanatical. Just take some wise precautions.

Another valuable investment on this same level is food storage. Get the kind that lasts many years and keep it in a cool, dry place. Many people store guns and bullets with their food and metal coins. Learning to hunt might be a very helpful preparation. Again, this is for last-ditch survival needs, but having it as part of your investment hierarchy can be very valuable.

PUT SOME MONEY INTO PREPARING FOR A WORST-CASE SCENARIO. DON'T BE FANATICAL ABOUT THIS, BUT DON'T IGNORE IT EITHER.

Level Four: Long-Term and Targeted Savings

After you have enough in your emergency fund to cover three to six months of living expenses and you have a solid survival preparation reserve, you can move up the hierarchy and invest in your long-term savings. This is still *your* money, the money you pay yourself first and never spend. As your 10% (or more) from all income you receive accumulates, this investment becomes bigger and bigger.

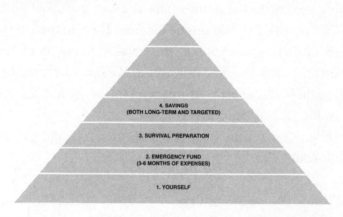

At this point, you can also create additional targeted savings accounts for the things you want to buy in the future. This is what most people consider typical "savings," the kind your parents probably taught you about. It consists of money you plan to spend later, unlike the 10% you pay yourself first—which you never use on consumer spending.

BUILD UP A REGULAR TARGETED SAVINGS FUND FOR THINGS YOU WANT TO BUY LATER. CONSISTENTLY FUND THIS ACCOUNT AND BUY CONSUMER ITEMS WITH CASH (NOT FINANCING).

Building up a targeted savings fund enables you to save ahead so you can always pay cash instead of using credit to finance things such as cars, college for your kids, a new house you want to buy or build some day, a trip, or investment money for your kids to build a business of their own when they become adults, etc.

If you have no debt, the goal would be to ramp up the amount you pay yourself from 10% to higher amounts. Orrin recommends setting the financial goal of reducing expenses and increasing income to the point where you can live off of no more than 75% of your net, take-home income. Then, in the long term, as your finances grow, you can go down to living off of 50% of your income. Imagine how full your YOU, Inc. Investment Hierarchy could be, securing your financial future, by not blowing all your money the moment it is received.

To clarify, each time we receive income, for example, we do the following:

- We put 10% toward tithing.
- We put 10% (or more) toward our YOU, Inc. Investment Hierarchy to fulfill the "pay yourself first" principle.
- We give something to offerings/charity.
- If we are in debt, we pay as much as we can outside of the 10% we pay ourselves toward our debt.
- If we have no debt, we put some money toward a targeted savings fund (for a car, trip, etc.), or we increase the 10% we pay ourselves to a higher percentage of our income.
- We pay our bills and live off the rest of the income (using the cash envelope method discussed earlier if needed—see the workbook for more details).

Note that by this point, we are down to just three more levels of investment, and most everything we have covered so far could legitimately be called "savings." Note, too, that the base of the hierarchy is bigger at the bottom to show the greater importance of those foundational steps, not necessarily to indicate that the *amounts* of money at those levels are larger than later (or higher) steps in the hierarchy.

This is a key point: Leaders are savers. They invest in things that last. People who invest in things that are unsecure and unsafe usually don't have much money and are frequently caught in a continuous cycle of financial struggles. Follow this program and become an accomplished saver.

A Warning

It is essential not to speculate with your savings. Use your savings in the ways listed in the first four levels of the YOU, Inc. Investment Hierarchy. It's called savings for a reason; do not ever speculate with it.

In fact, if you never invested in anything above the first four levels, you could do very, very well financially. For example, a report in *U.S. News & World Report* summarized Warren Buffett's investing method as follows:

- Research extensively.
- Buy what you know.
- Resist peer pressure.
- Shun risk.
- Learn from your mistakes.
- Eliminate debt.[13]

We wholeheartedly agree with these excellent guidelines. Be very careful investing beyond the first four levels of the YOU, Inc. Investment Hierarchy because this is the point at which we begin allowing RISK into the formula.

Level Five: Secure Investments

The fifth level of investment is to invest in something extremely secure, such as CDs, money market accounts, and municipal bonds. Many investment advisors downplay these investments because they pay very low interest, but, significantly, they also have lower risk.

ONLY INVEST MONEY YOU CAN AFFORD TO LOSE ENTIRELY IN SPECULATIONS OUTSIDE YOUR AREA(S) OF MASTERY. ONLY INVEST A LITTLE, IF ANY, IN SUCH VENTURES.

Note: Your big returns should come from Level One, investments in yourself and your business, not from Level Five or higher. Only put a little money into Level Five, and only put into Levels Six and Seven what you can afford to lose completely.

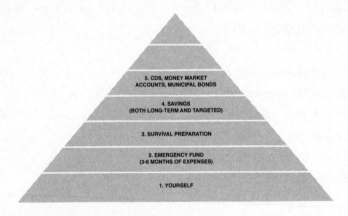

Level Six: Real Estate and Stocks

This level consists of investments in real estate and the stock market (including mutual funds). For many people, the best advice is to largely avoid these investments. The one exception is if your business is found in these arenas. If so, pay the price to attain real mastery in these areas (the 10,000 hours discussed earlier). Get the right mentors, learn from trial and error, and become a master.

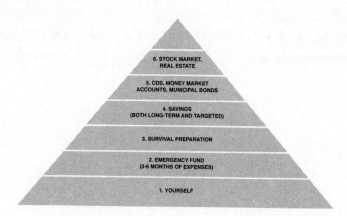

If neither real estate nor the stock market is your area of mastery, only put money into these arenas if you have already fully funded the previous levels of the hierarchy and can also afford to lose the full amount of your investment. And only put a little here. Levels Six and Seven are speculative and should always be treated as such.

Above all, never sign for something where you are liable for more than your own responsibility. There are a number of investments that follow this pattern, and they are poison. Those who sell the investment may seem very capable, but don't ever give away your financial freedom this way.

In all investments, especially as you increase in your financial fitness, always remember to strive to earn like the wealthy and live like the middle class (in terms of the relationship between your earning and spending). Frugality is wise, and it encourages more happiness than excessive spending or speculative investing.

Level Seven: Other Speculation

The final level of the hierarchy includes other areas of speculation. As you make more money, you will become a target for those seeking investors. Always take the time to really research and think through all investments you are considering. As we said about Level Six, those who promote investments frequently appear to be very capable, but do not act until you have gotten numerous credible opinions and studied it from every angle.

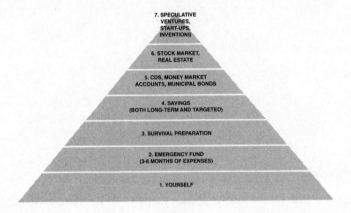

Levels One through Four are basically savings and are the principal steps of investing in yourself, while Levels Five through Seven are speculation. The rule of thumb is to minimize investing in anything (except the first four levels) outside your area of mastery. There are just too many nuances and details that those without mastery of the field do not understand. So if real estate is your primary business, for example, gain true mastery in it and invest in it. In such a case, real estate would be Level One. For anyone else, real estate is on Level Six.

In short, investing outside your area of mastery is often unwise. Even if such investments turn out to be profitable, they are nearly always very complicated and time-consuming. They require you to divide your focus and not pay as much attention to your own business or your life purpose and the reason you are trying to become financially fit in the first place.

REMEMBER: Avoid speculative ventures outside your area of mastery. Distraction detracts from your most significant actions. Be careful dividing yourself.

Orrin wrote the following:

As the old saying goes, "A fool and his money are soon parted." Achieving financial success in one field requires consistently applying the right strategies. However, even when one has accomplished the task, it doesn't make one an expert in all money-making endeavors. Because the world is filled with business opportunities, a person would be wise to stay focused within his or her field of expertise. Focus, in other words, is one of the keys for long-term success.

Despite reading and understanding these concepts, Chris and I confirmed them firsthand. A few older gentlemen, whom we had heard give excellent speeches about leadership, called us and asked us to invest in a "sure thing" as silent partners. I told them that neither of us were experts in the restaurant field and therefore would probably not be interested.

Sadly, after numerous phone calls, my resolve broke and we invested. The restaurant group proceeded to build over ten restaurants within a couple of years. No one was managing the numbers properly and operation cost was exceeding cash flow every month. We didn't know the business sector well enough to know if the numbers were normal or problematic, and we were assured that everything was going well.

To make matters worse, even though both Chris and I objected to signing personal guarantees, this was glossed over as merely a formality and we were told that the properties would be worth more than our guarantees.

After losing several million dollars for five years in a row, we finally got out of the mess and now feel qualified to give sound advice in this area. Do NOT, I repeat, do not use hard-earned money from one field that you *do* understand to finance someone's pet project in a field where you *haven't* gained mastery. Unless you yourself are minding the business, chances are that others will not apply the same intensity, resolve, and attention to detail you applied to making your money in the first place.

DO NOT EVER USE YOUR SAVINGS TO SPECULATE.

Friends and Family

There is also a special case where family and friends are concerned. As you increase in prosperity, those close to you will naturally see you as an investor for their projects. If you are considering loaning money to friends and family, just give it to them instead. Otherwise, you are setting yourself up for disappointment and relationship problems. If their projects bring a return, you can be pleasantly surprised. But they seldom do, so just give them the money outright, or simply tell them, "No." Whatever problems might be caused by not investing in their plans will be far less than investing with the expectation of an actual financial return.

Overall Investment Guidelines

Remember that there are going to be economic ups and downs, bursting bubbles and stock market shifts, wars and rumors of wars, deaths and illnesses, accidents and layoffs, and other unexpected challenges, so the key to financial success is to make the principles in this book into habits.

These habits are the best investment in your finances. Form good financial habits and stick to them. Put them on autopilot so you can focus on things beyond finances in your life.

This approach may not seem as sexy or cool as those suggested in many investment books and late night "get–rich–quick" infomercials, but it works. The others seldom do.

So Let It Be Written

Add what you have learned in this chapter to your written financial plan. Then apply these principles of financial fitness.

Summary of Part II—Offense

- Financial offense means taking action to increase your income. This is the first focus of financial fitness beyond the basics because it emphasizes the attitudes of abundance, leadership, innovation, and entrepreneurialism.

- The principles of financial offense covered in Part II are:

  - PRINCIPLE 8: People with the right moneyview discipline themselves to live the principles of financial fitness, make financial decisions based on a long-term vision, adopt the habit of delayed gratification, and use the compounding nature of money to constructively achieve their dreams.

  - PRINCIPLE 9: Financially fit people are avid readers and consistently invest in themselves by increasing their financial and leadership education, skills, experience, knowledge, and ability.

  - PRINCIPLE 10: Financially fit people excel at the work and projects they are doing now, and at the same time, they invest in themselves in order to achieve their long-term vision.

  - PRINCIPLE 11: Never sacrifice principles for money or possessions. Be honest. Keep your integrity. Keep your priorities in the right order.

  - PRINCIPLE 12: Do the work to gain mastery in what you do (usually about 10,000 hours).

  - PRINCIPLE 13: Financially fit people don't ask "Can we afford it?" as much as they ask "Do we *really* want this? Will it help our purpose and dream? *How* will it help our purpose and dream? In what ways might it be a distraction? Will it cost more money to take care of it or keep it (through things like insurance or annual fees)? Would saving or investing the same amount be a bigger help to our purpose and vision? Is *now* the best time for this purchase, or would it be less expensive or just better for our family or business at a later date?" They cultivate a habit of saying "No" to purchases even when they can easily afford them and of putting much of their money into savings or investments instead.

- > PRINCIPLE 14: Financially fit people analyze their habits—in life as well as finances—and work to break bad habits and cultivate good ones. They think about and choose the habits they want and need to achieve their life dreams.

- > PRINCIPLE 15: Own a business, even if you start out working on it part-time. You can apply all the other principles in this book and obtain wealth over time, but those who apply them in their own businesses can become wealthy much more quickly.

- > PRINCIPLE 16: Increase your passive income to the point that 1) most of your income is passive and 2) you can live off your passive income.

- > PRINCIPLE 17: Retirement should not be an issue of age but rather a function of having enough passive income to live on for life. Retirement means retiring from things that are not part of your purpose so you can focus your productive work on your life mission.

- > PRINCIPLE 18: To really attain financial success, focus on these things: 1) Truly excel in your current job and projects and simultaneously start a business, 2) Put in the 10,000 or so hours needed to gain mastery over your business while still excelling at your current job, 3) Make a plan to become financially free by reaching a point where the passive income from your business more than covers your family's needs, and 4) Once you are financially free, put your full-time focus on building your business to the point that it funds your life purpose. Each of these requires deep focus, one at a time. Once you have accomplished one of them, go to the next and give it the same level of focus.

> PRINCIPLE 19: Get good mentors and really listen to them.

> PRINCIPLE 20: Use your money productively—by putting it where it will bring you back more than you put in—rather than nonproductively. The best investment is in yourself and your own business. Wisely and appropriately use some of your savings to increase your business assets and returns.

> PRINCIPLE 21: Put some money into preparing for a worst-case scenario. Don't be fanatical about this, but don't ignore it either.

> PRINCIPLE 22: Build up a regular targeted savings fund for things you want to buy later. Consistently fund this account and buy consumer items with cash (not financing).

> PRINCIPLE 23: Only invest money you can afford to lose entirely in speculations outside your area(s) of mastery. Only invest a little, if any, in such ventures.

> PRINCIPLE 24: Do not ever use your savings to speculate.

• Be sure to stop and consider how to use all of these principles in your life, and add them to your written financial plan.

DEFENSE

"GET THE QUARTER BACK!"

It is said that the best offense is a good defense, and vice versa, and in the game of football, the first focus of defense is to get the quarterback. Imagine if you could literally have back every quarter you have ever had in your life. How much money would that be in your bank account right now? In Part III, we will learn the principles of caring for your resources and protecting against loss and decline. Defense builds on the earlier principles of financial fitness and ensures that you can live your dreams.

Try to become not a man of success, but try rather to become a man of value.
—ALBERT EINSTEIN

One of the greatest pieces of economic wisdom is to know what you do not know.
—JOHN KENNETH GALBRAITH

SIXTEEN

Myths about Debt

I'll trade you one dollar for five dollars.
—JAROD KINTZ

Let's begin this chapter with a multiple-choice question. The quote above comes from which of the following?

A. A government agency
B. A marketing ad for a new credit card
C. A comedian

The answer is C, a comedian, but it could easily have come from any marketing campaign for buying something with credit. When we make purchases with debt, we end up paying more (frequently *a lot* more) than the item originally cost.

Nobody likes being in debt, but ironically, almost everyone has too much experience with it. If you are in debt, you face a kind of financial slavery. Anyone who has stayed awake most of the night feeling the chest pain of overwhelming debt knows how important it is to be financially fit. The first focus of financial defense is to get rid of debt as quickly as possible.

GET RID OF DEBT.

Major Myths

There are a number of myths surrounding debt. One is that debt is a great tool used to create prosperity. It isn't. It's one of the main things holding back financial success of all kinds. Those who suggest that debt is an important tool for creating wealth are mixing up their realities. Yes, debt as investment leverage can be a positive multiplier when done in the confines of the investment category (covered earlier), but too often people use this as an excuse to use consumer debt.

Specifically, business debt may at some point be helpful in advancing a project, but this is the exception rather than the rule. And even in such cases, finding a way to do it without debt is almost always better than using the debt approach. And consumer debt, as we discussed earlier, is never good.

Sadly, people frequently buy something on credit that is actually a consumer purchase rationalizing that it has a business purpose and that it is therefore okay to use debt. This is a serious problem for a lot of people.

IF YOU AREN'T FINANCIALLY SOUND, DON'T GET CAUGHT IN THE TRAP OF USING "BUSINESS DEBT."

The rule is that debt is bad. Avoid it in nearly every situation. The only possible exceptions are the purchase of a home (more on this later) or legitimate business debt where financing is the best option. Note that those who use business debt effectively are nearly always financially fit enough that they really understand when and where debt is useful. If you haven't attained lasting financial fitness, you are not at this level.

Another myth about debt is that you should build your credit with a credit card. This is a temptation to get into massive debt. In fact, this dangerous course of action is most often recommended to young people or to people who have declared bankruptcy, and these are precisely the people who should not have credit cards.

Building your credit is best accomplished by saving, always being prepared for emergencies (by having an emergency fund), paying your bills on time without fail, and making enough money to cover your needs and put some away. If you actually use a credit card and pay it off entirely every single month without exception, it will certainly build your credit. But 95% of people who use the "credit cards build my credit" excuse just end up getting themselves into more debt. Do not fall into this trap. That being said, a credit card can be used as a vital tool to help you function in society and make it easier to get rental cars, hotel rooms, etc., but doing this does require discipline. Also, if you have good credit and discipline, credit cards serve as perfectly acceptable emergency backup funds to cushion you against unexpected financial blows.

DO NOT USE CREDIT CARDS TO BUILD YOUR CREDIT BECAUSE THIS ALMOST ALWAYS LEADS PEOPLE TO MORE DEBT.

More Debt Myths

Other myths about debt include the idea that the following are good financial choices:

- Title pawning
- "Ninety-days-same-as-cash" loans
- Payday loans
- Rent-to-own plans
- Layaway debt

Anything like these is a bad idea—like a chocolate-covered hand grenade! These are the financial fitness equivalents of chocolate candy bars and cotton candy. They are very, very bad for you. They are not even really financial food; they are fake finances, and they get you in more trouble every time.

Avoid these like the plague. Find other ways, or deny yourself.

NEVER USE TITLE PAWNING, "NINETY-DAYS-SAME-AS-CASH" LOANS, PAYDAY LOANS, RENT-TO-OWN PLANS, LAYAWAY DEBT, OR SIMILAR SCHEMES.

We understand that sometimes you simply have to use credit, like when a child gets sick or is hurt and you don't have your emergency fund built up yet. In such circumstances, you may need to use your credit cards. But even in such circumstances, these "pawning" loan kind of schemes should be totally avoided.

Myths about Car Loans

Perhaps the biggest myths regarding debt deal with car loans. This is also one way to clearly identify whether you are on the path to financial fitness or headed in the other direction.

People who use credit to purchase cars are on a road to financial struggles. Do not use car debt. The myths say that financing a car is okay, but it isn't. Find another way. Buy your car used. Plan ahead and save up so you can pay cash. Drive around an old clunker until you have cash for something better.

This is a brain issue because some people think new cars are the only things worth buying. If you can pay cash for a new car, great, but as the researchers who wrote *The Millionaire Next Door* found, the large majority of people who can actually (easily) afford a new car don't buy one. They buy used cars with low miles. And they pay cash.

They do this because they see vehicles as transportation, not as status symbols or shiny new baubles. If you want to be financially fit, follow their example.

SEE YOUR CAR(S) AS TRANSPORTATION, NOT STATUS SYMBOLS. SAVE UP AND ALWAYS PAY CASH FOR THEM.

Work to put your mindset in the right place concerning cars. They are transportation. They are not business investments. They are not status symbols, except in the sense that they create a feeling of false status where the owner looks good to the lower classes but is actually broke.

Furthermore, do not buy into the marketing myths about leasing. Just buy and pay cash. Leasing cars is a great way to just throw away money. The car loses about 25% of its value in the first year, and they make the person leasing the car pay for this depreciation. Then they hammer him with exorbitant costs for extra miles and other fees.

In the same vein, do not get sucked in by marketing campaigns like 0% interest loans. You might think that you are saving money by not having to pay interest, but you will still be hammered with the loss of value the moment you drive the car off the lot. Plus, debt is debt, and cars are not worth debt.

Remember, debt is slavery. A car bought on debt will wear out faster than most people can pay it off. This means that within months, the car will no longer be a new, shiny status symbol, but you will have to keep working to pay for it even after it is no longer exciting.

The myths about car debt have kept a lot of people from becoming financially fit. Do not get bamboozled by these myths. They're myths, after all! Be wise about your transportation choices. This will be a huge benefit to becoming financially fit.

If you really want a certain car, fine. Follow the other principles of financial fitness and save up money so you can pay cash for it. This is the way of financial success.

For example, well into his business career, Chris set a goal to get a convertible Corvette. He chose to leverage his desire to hit some business and financial goals before allowing himself the purchase. In that way, buying the Corvette would be a reward for achievement instead of an indulgence of materialism.

After about nine months, Chris had accomplished both the business goals and financial goals to get the car. But he waited. He was still excited about the acquisition, but he wanted to take his time to find just the right one. Six more months passed. Then one day as he drove past the Chevy dealership, he spotted the exact car he wanted for sale in a long line of Corvettes.

Incredibly, it was also on sale for a huge discount. Chris made the purchase in less than ten minutes. What looked abrupt and spontaneous to the car dealer was actually the work of almost a year and a half. By setting up the purchase of the car in this way, Chris was able to not only gain leverage on himself for higher performance, but also to develop a patience that ended up saving him thousands of dollars on the purchase.

Three More Big Money Myths

Another huge myth is that credit cards are safer than debit cards, and that you must have a credit card in order to fly, get a hotel room, or rent a car. Debit cards are excellent for this instead. They debit cash. And as long as you are following the financial principles already covered in this book, you will be able to wisely manage your debit card.

In fact, if you are applying the principles covered so far in this book, you probably have the discipline to use a credit card just for travel expenses and then fully pay off the card every month. In other words, you may be able to use a credit card as a debit card. If not, use a debit card.

The key is to pay for things right now. Pay as you go.

Credit marketing firms have also tried to convince our society that we should give credit cards to kids, the younger the better, so they can learn to use debt. This is another hurtful myth. Most youth simply learn to spend, spend, spend—and leave it to adults to bail them out. This is the opposite of teaching them good financial fitness.

> **The key is to pay for things right now. Pay as you go.**

DEBIT CARDS ARE BETTER THAN CREDIT CARDS FOR MANY PEOPLE, AND CASH IS EVEN BETTER.

Youth can learn by using cash, checks, or even, eventually, a debit card. Prepaid credit cards can also work. Explain the principles of financial success to them, and meet with them every week or month to balance their checkbook, record of cash used, or debit card statement. Have them read this book and learn the forty-seven fundamentals of financial fitness while they are young, and then help them follow the principles.

TEACH YOUR CHILDREN AND YOUTH THE PRINCIPLES OF FINANCIAL FITNESS. SET THE EXAMPLE FOR THEM. MENTORING THEM WILL HELP YOU AS WELL AS THEM.

The Inside Scoop on Second Mortgages

Another serious financial myth is that second mortgages constitute good financial policy. This follows the same principle as business debt: If you are wealthy, you might use a second mortgage for some wise purpose. Everyone else should entirely avoid second mortgages.

IF YOU ARE NOT WEALTHY, DO NOT GET SUCKED IN TO USING SECOND MORTGAGES.

And, in reality, nearly all who are wealthy avoid them as well.

So Let It Be Done!

Determine how you are going to apply all the principles from this chapter, and add your intentions to your written financial plan.

SEVENTEEN

Getting Out of Debt

*The man who does more than he is paid for will soon
be paid for more than he does.*
—NAPOLEON HILL

The day you pay off the last of your debt will be one of the most important in your life. Hopefully, your children and grandchildren will never have to have this experience because they will learn and live the principles of financial fitness based on your example, and as a result, they will not ever go into debt.

If you are already in debt, however, the day you pay it off will be a great memory. You may shed tears, you may leap high in the air and give a loud whoop, or you might find yourself offering prayers of thanks. Maybe you'll do all three, as many people have when they have found themselves released from financial slavery.

This isn't to say that being in debt is as bad as actual slavery, but when most people get out of debt, it feels as if a million-pound weight has been lifted from around their neck.

For example, Nick and Kelly just could not seem to get ahead, though they were working several jobs. They worried about paying all the bills for their children and family. They were in debt and struggling to get their finances in order and had gone through job losses and periods of unemployment when they came across the material contained in this book.

They decided to do whatever it took to learn the discipline necessary to get out of debt. They made hard decisions and cut as much of their spending from their budget as they could. They even sold some prized possessions, including a special full-sized Spider-Man collectible that Nick had cherished for years, in order to pay off their debts.

"That was hard," he said. "My friends all knew I loved that Spider-Man, but we had decided to get out of debt, and we were prepared to do what we had to do to stick to our commitment."

In a little over a year and a half, Nick and Kelly totally eliminated their debt and were living an entirely cash lifestyle. Kelly was able to stay at home full-time with her children, as she had always desired to do. "It's so much better to be in charge of your finances instead of having them in charge of you," said Kelly.

The Roll-Down Method

But exactly how do you get out of debt? The answer is simple. In fact, if you are living the principles we have already covered in this book, it will actually be pretty straightforward. If not, if you are still avoiding the principles of financial fitness, getting out of debt might be very difficult for you.

Here is how it works. First, even if you have debt, you still pay yourself 10% of your income, but no more than this amount. Paying yourself first and paying tithes and offerings have taught you discipline. In short, you know how to put away money, deny yourself, and live within your means. And you do not increase your debt because you don't use consumer debt anymore—at all. By applying the principles in this book, you are changing your heart and mind to an attitude of financial fitness. This makes getting out of debt a lot simpler (and likely) than if you hadn't developed any of these habits. So pat yourself on the back for having obtained these positive habits of financial success. That is the first step.

Second, pay off your consumer debt, especially credit cards. The interest on cards is high, and paying them off is essential. Use the skills you have learned from saving and apply them now to getting rid of debt.

The idea of the debt roll-down method is simple: List your cards in order from the smallest balance to the largest. If there is a choice between two low-balance cards, pay the one with the highest interest off first. The goal is to get rid of the clutter of all the smallest payments and kill off the easiest debts first. Decide on a fixed percentage or amount of money that you are able to add every month to your minimum debt payments and make this as automatic as possible.

If you are saving money in a targeted savings account for a specific planned purchase, you can stop putting money there for a few months to help pay off this card.

If you receive any windfalls of cash or unexpected income, add it to the lowest balance card. Sell things from your garage or storage, or other things you do not need. The goal is to knock out the balance on the card as quickly as possible.

Identify three things you usually buy and deny yourself these things until you have paid off this card. Put the money you would have spent on these three items directly to your card. This could include coffee, soft drinks, candy bars, or other treats, eating out for the next two months, getting your nails done, the extra cell phone in your household, or something else.

Maybe you can carpool to work to save on fuel or only drive to town once a week instead of whenever it occurs to you. Use the skills you learned earlier when you were focused on saving, things like getting on the same page with your spouse and saying "No" in the short term in order to achieve your long-term goals.

The Next Step

Third, once you have paid off the first card, keep the same amount going toward the card with the next lowest balance. Give this a similar focus and pay off this card as soon as possible. To be clear, every time you pay a card off, you add what you were paying on that card to the next card payment. So, as you pay off a debt and roll down the payment to the next one, you pick up momentum. Continue to do the same with each card until all of your credit card debt is gone. At that point, apply this same roll-down method to your other debts, starting with those that have the highest interest rates.

USE THE ROLL-DOWN METHOD TO PAY OFF ALL CREDIT CARD DEBTS AND THEN APPLY IT TO ALL OTHER DEBTS.

The chart below shows an example of a monthly payment schedule with the debt roll-down method.

	Debt 1	Debt 2	Debt 3	Debt 4	Debt 5
Month 1	$50	$130	$225	$250	$300
Month 2	$50	$130	$225	$250	$300
Month 3	$50	$130	$225	$250	$300
Month 4	$50	$130	$225	$250	$300
Month 5	*➡	$180	$225	$250	$300
Month 6		$180	$225	$250	$300
Month 7		$180	$225	$250	$300
Month 8		$180	$225	$250	$300
Month 9		$180	$225	$250	$300
Month 10		*➡	$405	$250	$300
Month 11			$405	$250	$300
Month 12			$405	$250	$300
Month 13			$405	$250	$300
Month 14			$405	$250	$300
Month 15			*➡	$250	$300
Month 16				$655	$300
Month 17				$655	$300
Month 18				$655	$300
Month 19				$655	$300
Month 20				$655	$300
Month 21				*➡	$955
Month 22					$955

*As each debt is paid off, the payment amount is added to the next debt payment to the right.

Below is a copy of the Debt Roll-Down form available in the workbook. This example shows a list of debts in order from the smallest to the largest balance. The total amount of the minimum payments equals $440. Once the first card has been paid off, the $20 that was being paid to that debt gets added to the second debt payment. The new payment (which is always the total of the previous debts' payments plus the current debt's payment) for the second is now $60, and $440 is still paid toward the total debt. The sample below shows what your form will look like as debts are paid off:

Debt Roll-Down

Item	Balance Owed	Minimum Payment	Interest Rate	New Payment
Department Store	$500	$20	18%	$20
Furniture Store	$1,000	$40	22%	$60
MasterCard	$2,000	$80	19%	$140
American Express	$3,000	$120	19%	$260
Visa	$4,500	$180	20%	$440

Without the debt roll-down method, it would take you thirteen years to pay off these debts, and you would pay $7,139 in interest. Using the debt roll-down method, it would take you only *two years and nine months* to pay them off, and you would save *$3,890* in interest!

This example uses only the minimum payments. Imagine how much faster this roll-down method could go if a set amount of money was added every month. If an extra $50 a month was added to this example, it would be paid off in two years and six months and would save you $4,275 in interest. With an extra $100 every month, it would be paid off in two years and three months and would save you $4,578 in interest. And adding an extra $200 every month would enable you to pay it off in one year and ten months while saving almost $5,000 in interest.

The roll-down method allows you to reduce debt more quickly because your minimum payments go away when a card is paid off and that amount goes toward paying off the principal of the next card. As we mentioned before, if it took you ten years to get into debt, it might take ten to fix it. But with the roll-down method, you will do it as quickly as possible.

Also, by focusing on financial offense and the principles from Part I and Part II of this book, you'll naturally see increased income that will help in this process. This isn't automatic, of course, given the ups and downs of the economy, but if you're applying all the principles so far in this book, your efforts to get out of debt will be significantly multiplied.

One of the great things about the principles of financial fitness is that as you apply more of them, the others often become easier. There is a synergy that occurs as you follow more and more of these principles.

For example, Marc and Kristine Militello experienced an amazing financial turnaround by applying sound principles of financial fitness. Marc was a teacher and a coach, while Kristine stayed home to raise their four children, ages seven and younger, including a newborn baby. They made around $75,000 a year, but they had $106,000 of debt. In fact, their stove only had one working burner, and their refrigerator was so old that the brackets were broken and they had to buy dowels to put under the shelves in order to hold the food. Their home was 1,000 square feet, and they struggled to pay all their bills.

This reality would be a challenge for most people, but as Marc put it, "When we started digging ourselves out of debt, we didn't have a lot of money; we just had to start where we were with what we had."

The first thing they did was write down everything they spent for thirty days—everything, even a dime. They found that their big money wasters were grabbing a soda or snack at the gas station and losing track of how much they were spending because they simply swiped their debit cards at drive-thru fast food places.

They brainstormed ways to avoid these expenses, including taking snacks with them when they went out in order to skip the fast food and putting dinner in a crock pot early in the day so they wouldn't be tempted to order pizza for dinner.

Then they made themselves face the brutal reality of their expenses and develop an effective initial budget. Marc said, "Without writing down exactly what you spend for a month, your budget will be flawed from the beginning. After creating an initial budget, we divided our money up for each spending area and put it in envelopes. We marked each legal-sized envelope with the amount of money and the purpose of the money. Then we wrote down what we spent each time we used money from the envelope—and we wrote the expense right there on the envelope for each other to see."

Kristine said:

> Doing this taught me how truly bad I was with the money. I could see firsthand what I was doing with money—shifting it around and not sticking to the parameters. For example, I would go over on groceries, so I would take it from gas. Then at the end of the week, I would be out of gas money and would need to borrow more from some other envelope.
>
> It showed me how I wasn't sticking to the budget. If you truly have a budget problem, a few weeks of legitimately going over the budget will clearly show that the allotted amount of money is wrong and needs to be ad-

justed. However, most times the problem is simply a matter of not sticking with the allotted amount of money.

During this time, we used absolutely no debit cards, just the cash and the big envelopes, because before that, we really had no idea what we were spending. I understand a person can go home and check the bank statements online and calculate spending. The problems with this approach are: 1) Expenses don't always post immediately, and 2) By the time the bill comes, it's too late, and you've spent more on other things.

Think of the cash envelope system as training wheels. After a few months of doing this, you can know what you actually do spend and need, and you are ready to create a solid, immoveable budget. The key is that someone has to stick to it and be the stone wall, and the other has to follow. If the line is moveable, you will never learn to stay inside it.

> "A budget is not a line drawn in the sand. It is a stone wall."
> —Kristine Militello

A budget is not a line drawn in the sand. It is a stone wall.

Marc added:

Plug the holes in the boat: Stop spending money you don't have! Remove emotion and just do the right thing. You can't even understand the basis of your wants and needs until you do all these steps. Without an understanding of what you have or don't have, you can't or won't even realize you're spending on emotion.

Once you understand how much you have and where it all needs to go, then you truly understand what you are doing with money. Now you can clearly ask yourself if it's a want or a need. More money doesn't fix the problem until you really understand your finances and take charge of them.

> "More money doesn't fix the problem until you really understand your finances and take charge of them."
> —Marc Militello

Over time, with a lot of hard work and personal discipline, Marc and Kristine applied the principles of financial success and became financially fit. Today, they live in a big home on three acres and drive a Mercedes and a Cadillac. As Marc summarized their experience: "I can hardly believe it myself." The principles of financial fitness work.

Getting Help

It is possible to consolidate your debts onto one card so that you pay less in minimum payments and can apply more toward the principal in every payment. Some cards allow you to transfer balances from other cards at no charge. But these debt consolidation techniques can be very dangerous and are only for those who are very disciplined. When the debts are consolidated into a smaller monthly payment, many people end up using the extra money to buy more things with debt and get into an even deeper hole.

There are companies that help people consolidate and make automatic payments to reduce debt. Be careful with such companies, however. Some are outright scams, and others charge exorbitant fees. But if you have a hard time following through with paying off your cards and other debts every time you are paid, getting help might be your best plan. Whatever it takes, pay off your credit cards, keep saving, stick to a budget, do not use any more consumer debt, and utilize the roll-down method to get out of debt.

Sometimes creditors will negotiate a deal with someone who can come up with a sum of money, even if it is smaller than the balance owed. Often a large balance can be paid off for a lower amount.

Put It into Practice

Make sure you put this plan to get out of debt into action right away. This one thing will drastically improve your finances.

EIGHTEEN

Don't Be Normal

If you were offered the chance to live your own life again,
would you seize the opportunity?
—CHRISTOPHER HITCHENS

Normal people are broke. Don't be normal where finances are concerned. Normal people trust their emotions about money, and as a result, their finances are a disaster.

Do not trust your emotions about money, especially about spending and using debt. There is a "True North," a reality, a best way to use money, and people's emotions are seldom aligned with this truth. This is why having a financial mentor can help you so much in gaining financial fitness, and why knowing and following the principles of financial fitness—rather than your emotions or old habits—is essential.

So don't be normal when it comes to money. Be the exception, one of the few who understands and applies these principles consistently—always.

> **Normal people are broke. Don't be normal where finances are concerned.**

If you are exceptional where money is concerned, you will have exceptional financial fitness and live an exceptional life mission. Do not settle for mediocrity. Live the greatness you were born to live! Become the leader God means you to be.

The Two Big Roadblocks

There are two main things that keep most people from being exceptional with money and living exceptional life dreams. The first comes from mental blocks, misunderstandings, and false beliefs that hold you back and keep you from success.

If you find yourself disagreeing with any of the principles of financial success listed in this book, you are on dangerous ground. Sadly, there are a lot of financial fads out there. Pay them no attention. The principles in this book work. Don't get distracted by financial fads. Stick to the solid, proven principles of financial fitness.

A second major reason people do not reach financial fitness is that they are swayed by the massive power of marketing and media. Companies spend millions of dollars hiring brilliant marketers who figure out how to get people to buy their products and services—even when they can't afford them and even when they must use debt to make the purchases.

The messages and advertising campaigns they promote influence and can even change how people think. Many governments even get in the game by reinforcing these beliefs and encouraging increased consumer spending and debt.

Some tax codes make it worse by penalizing savings (i.e., if you save the money, you pay taxes on it, but if you spend it on certain things—like a big truck or SUV—it can often be written off as an expense; also, mortgage tax deductions incentivize buying a home, even when a family can't really afford it).

The sheer weight of so much marketing and incentivizing is hard for many people to withstand. Again, to be financially exceptional, you can't just be normal.

LEARN TO BE SKEPTICAL OF ADVERTISING, MEDIA, AND MARKETING.

The Rule of Your Top Five

Understanding the Rule of Your Top Five Friends can be a powerful boost to your finances. People tend toward what they see modeled by their closest friends, and there is an old saying in business that your finances will tend to reflect the average of the financial fitness of your five closest friends.

While this isn't always accurate for every person, the general principle is still true. If you spend your time with people who value spending and the ideas promoted by our marketing culture (like using debt to get what you want right now or impressing your friends by only buying designer-label clothes and new cars), their bad habits will most likely rub off on you.

In contrast, if your closest friends value savings, having no debt, business growth, leadership, abundance, giving, service, delayed gratification, and investing in quality things that are assets rather than just expenses, their enthusiasm will probably influence you—and your financial choices.

Regardless of who you spend your time with, becoming financially fit means adopting this second set of values and rejecting the first list.

When you are in the mindset of investment rather than spending, it is easier to apply the principles of financial fitness. Teaching the right values to your youth and children is very important because they are frequently bombarded with the Spending and Debt view of finances and life.

Again, being normal is a bad idea in a society where normal people are broke and deeply in debt. Find a way to be exceptional instead. To do this, learn to overcome the mental roadblocks and false money beliefs that are widespread in the world and reject the consumer culture that convinces most people to spend more and use debt.

In short, follow the principles of financial fitness, even though that is not what "normal" people do.

Accumulate Slowly

For example, those who understand financial fitness also know that it is important to accumulate slowly. More stuff makes life more complicated, and more expensive, not easier. Minimizing the stuff you own will help you become more financially fit.

STUFF
by Chris Brady

You've got it. We've got it. Seems that nearly everyone's got it—stuff, I mean. Stuff is the stuff that we have sitting around our houses, garages, and especially basements. Some people go so far as to have stuff stored in a separate facility across town, or at an in-law's house strewn across their front yard, or at any number of Auxiliary Stuff Storage Locations.

Rich people have stuff, and usually lots of it. Interestingly, though, even poor people seem to have lots of stuff, although stuff of a lesser quality or luster. Young people have stuff, too, but old people generally have even more stuff (out-of-style stuff, to be sure). Before you're even born, people are holding "showers" and giving you stuff.

Each year you'll celebrate your age, and they will give you more stuff. And after you're gone, they'll bicker over the stuff you've left behind.

In our own home, we have stuff stored behind other stuff. Some stuff sits on top of other stuff, while other stuff just hides behind stuff. Some stuff is stuffed behind stuff, while still other stuff is out on display. But the older we get, the more we live, the more stuff we seem to have.

It's not all bad, really. Some stuff is pretty important. Take refrigerators, for instance. That's the kind of stuff that we all need—what's inside them, that is—and toilets and furniture and forks and cars and stamps and beds and a pretty huge, boring, and definitely too-long list of stuff that we actually need around.

But what drives me crazy is the rest of the stuff: the stuff that we just accumulate, like knick-knacks...tall ones and short ones, big ones and small, ugly ones and stylish things your wife got at the mall, dusty stuff and old stuff and broken stuff and kids' stuff, pet stuff and loaned stuff and present stuff and forgotten stuff.

Whenever I hear about someone who likes to shop, I picture a big pile of stuff. Isn't that really what shopping is, driving around trading money for more stuff? Drive it home and put it in amongst all your other stuff. And eventually, the total inventory of stuff gets quite overwhelming. This is because of the sticky nature of most stuff.

The most dangerous combination in a marriage is a shopper married to a pack rat. One makes a hobby out of buying stuff while the other refuses to part with stuff. The home of such a couple gets stuffed with stuff.

What can one do with all this stuff? Cram it and stuff it and store it and hide it. Or one can sell it. This is interesting because who in the world would want someone's stuff when everybody already has more than enough stuff of their own? I know. It is a perplexing puzzle, but people with stuff actually buy the stuff of other people with stuff at events called garage sales (although garages are not for sale), yard sales, or auctions. People line up to buy your stuff. They are even willing to pay twenty-six cents for stuff that cost you $450.

Or, you can give away some stuff. Pack it and wrap it and box it and donate it. The taxman will even give you a credit for giving away the stuff. This is so you will have more money to buy more stuff, and the government can tax the purchases and get money to buy stuff of its own, such as $600 toilet seats and $345 screwdrivers. Given this, it is easy to see why even the government has garage sales (called federal liquidations) once in while: to sell us the stuff they bought with the money they took from us when we bought our stuff. It's a stuff cycle of perpetual renown.

And that brings me to recycling. This is a concept where other people express concern over what you do with your stuff. (They don't care what you do with it while you possess it, only when you discard it.) They say some stuff should be ground up or melted or something and made into other stuff. It's another stuff cycle.

It seems, now that I have taken such an in-depth, scientific look into the nature of stuff that stuff is like a bad case of athlete's foot—very difficult to get rid of. Take a trip someplace, and there your wife is packing up all of your stuff. There are your kids, fighting over stuff. There's the robber, stealing someone's stuff. There's the envious, wanting another's stuff. There's the communist, confiscating stuff.

Try as you may through life, you will be forced to deal with stuff. Most of it looks pretty good when it's new, but just becomes stuff in a very short while. Maybe that's why they say the best stuff in life is stuff that's not even stuff.

Many financial advisors suggest holding a yard sale and getting rid of your extra stuff—and even some of the things you like but really don't need—as an essential part of getting financially in shape. The money from such sales can go directly to your $1,000 (and growing) beginning emergency fund.

Author Robert Kiyosaki refers to most purchases (cars, electronics, clothes, etc.) by the delightful, and accurate, name of "do-dads." People have too many worthless things in their homes, and getting

Reduce your stuff to make life less complicated.

rid of them by garage sale or even donation to charity frees up your mind and home for focus on the right things. Reduce your stuff to make life less complicated.

ACCUMULATE SLOWLY; BUILD YOUR INVENTORY OF RESOURCES AND WISDOM, NOT STUFF.

Even if you don't clear your life of clutter, at the very least, follow the principle of accumulating slowly. Do not be in a hurry to get more things. Focus instead on becoming a better leader and financial decision maker and on having more real *resources*. Accumulate wisdom faster than widgets.

> **Accumulate wisdom faster than widgets.**

Status Is a Terrible Trap

Also avoid the almost universal modern search for "status." Sadly, nowadays, having status often means that you look important and successful, but you are actually flat broke and deeply in debt.

People tend to get into this trap by spending money they don't have in an attempt to look good, "keep up with the Joneses," or impress people. Usually they don't even really like the people they are trying to impress.

This problem is frequently multiplied because in the attempt to "fit in," people buy many things they don't really need or want because such trappings seem to be socially "required." Sadly, such purchases are a lot less impressive than just living within your means, making no apology for where you are now because you are on a path toward success, applying the laws of financial fitness outlined in this book, and becoming financially fit, prosperous, and then wealthy.

Another word for seeking the wrong kind of status is *materialism*. If you pay attention, you'll notice that there are a lot of people who look like they are rich (big house, new cars, designer clothes, kids in private schools, etc.) but who are still living paycheck to paycheck—with a little help from Visa, Mastercard, American Express, Discover, and a few other "friends."

To become financially fit, you must make more than you spend and spend less than you make. In other words, you must live within your means. However you say it, the important thing is to live it, along with the other principles of financial fitness.

The principles of financial fitness work, but you have to apply them. If you get distracted trying to make people like you or accept you, three things will almost always happen: 1) They won't like you much anyway because they are interested in status rather than real friendship, 2) You won't like yourself all that much because you will be drowning in debt, and 3) You won't get out of your financial rut because you won't ever get around to applying the principles of financial fitness.

Even worse, you will never give the world the benefit of your great purpose and dream because you will be too busy trying to impress. This is a major waste of human capital. Worse, it's a waste of your life purpose.

The Status Fix

Founding Father John Adams wrote that nearly every person spends much of life trying to impress others.[14] He suggested not getting caught in this popular trap.

This was good advice when he gave it, and it is good advice now. The easiest, quickest fix to the status trap is to get right with God, live true principles in all areas of your life including finances, and then genuinely get to work on building the financial pipeline to your great life stewardship.

After all, if you're right with God, who else do you really need to impress? You want to serve others, yes, but impressing them just isn't your focus when you are busy applying true principles. Your duty to God is what really matters, and getting financially fit helps you better serve Him.

As business leader Claude Hamilton put it: "[T]he peace will come as you simply do what you know you should do. As you act from duty, you allow God to take care of your results. Only doing [things] for the money makes it hard

> **If you're right with God, who else do you really need to impress?**

189

and the time will come (yes, it will) that money will no longer motivate you. But sense of duty? That will."[15]

GET RIGHT WITH GOD, APPLY TRUE PRINCIPLES IN ALL AREAS OF LIFE INCLUDING FINANCES, PURSUE YOUR STEWARDSHIP, SERVE OTHERS—AND LEAVE IMPRESSING OTHERS IN GOD'S HANDS.

Materialism Hurts

Note that it is *not* materialism to dream of a better life for your family and your purpose. Dream big, and start living the principles that will make your dreams come true.

However, it *is* materialism to let *things* run your life. Just like communism is when the commune owns you or socialism occurs when the society owns the people, materialism happens when you are constantly working for the stuff and things in your life. You don't control your stuff in such situations; it controls you.

You go to work for it, you worry about it, you fight about it with those you love the most, and you do whatever is needed to keep it and get more of it. That is materialism because your stuff owns you.

By the way, the worst materialism happens when you buy the stuff on debt, use it up or wear it out, and then still have to work to pay it off. This is a pretty good definition of slavery. You have to work for the stuff, day in and day out, but you don't get to look forward to it at all because it is already gone.

But, in contrast, it is not materialism if your stuff works for you. If you buy it today with money you earned yesterday, you can sit back and really enjoy it. You can milk all the benefit and enjoyment from it, and it will not sidetrack you from your true purpose.

190

Debt does the opposite. Not only do you get to keep working for it long after you bought it, you actually work longer and harder to pay off the interest. And the anxiety, stress, and frustration of this arrangement always detracts from your real stewardship and dream.

After all, you have a pipeline to your dreams to build, and anything that blocks this isn't good for you. Debt is one of the biggest roadblocks of all. Make the proactive decision right now to not use consumer debt.

DO NOT USE CONSUMER DEBT. WISE FINANCING FOR BUSINESS INVESTMENT MAY BE OKAY AT TIMES, BUT CONSUMER DEBT IS LIKE A CANCER. CUT IT OUT!

If you are already in debt, it may take some time to repair what you broke. As we said before, if it took you ten years to become deeply in debt, it might take another ten to truly get out. So, yes, *materialism hurts.*

Sometimes, in order to take a step forward, you may have to take a couple steps back and downgrade your lifestyle. You may love your car, but its monthly payment might be killing you, and the same with other financed items, even your home. Selling such items and purchasing less expensive models can be helpful at times. Yes, this may be difficult to do. But remember, things are just things, and it's only temporary. If you follow the principles in this program and stay the course on your written financial plan, you will end up in a much better situation.

The good news is that if you apply the principles of financial fitness, when you do get out of debt, you will have a lot of other things going for you:

- A large amount of savings (following the YOU, Inc. Investment Hierarchy)
- A long history of tithing, giving, and serving
- The character and discipline to do what you know needs to be done financially, with the experience to back it up
- A business that you can grow to increase your passive income
- A life purpose that provides a powerful map for your choices
- An investment (rather than a spending) attitude
- A habit and the positive momentum of getting financially fit
- And so much more

Following these principles is powerful. By using them, you will have the power to totally fix and flourish your financial life.

Memories Matter

Another vital part of financial fitness is to put an accurate value on memories and relationships. Too many people put way too low a price tag on these things. Your budget needs to include money for making memories. These can be very simple, like taking a walk with your spouse, watching a sunset together, or taking the kids to the park for an hour. The little things are usually the best memories anyway.

MAKE MEMORIES PART OF YOUR LIFESTYLE, BUDGET, AND LIFE PLAN. START SIMPLE AND ADD BIG MEMORIES, TOO.

As you increasingly apply the principles of financial fitness and become more prosperous, make sure your "Memories" budget keeps pace. Go to the beach on three (or six) Hawaiian islands, take a month off and golf together if that is what you like, or take the family on an Alaskan safari. Read Chris's book *A Month of Italy* to get a full picture of a lifestyle built around creating greater family memories.

Chris summarizes this book as follows:

> At some point in the early winter of 2010, Terri and I decided we needed a break. We wanted a true "get away" where we could spend some quality and quantity family time, clear our heads, be together, and just think about our lives. It was only a nanosecond before I proposed Italy as the perfect destination because it was inexhaustibly interesting, historically attractive, climatically alluring, and sufficiently distant from our hectic lives as to offer just such the repose we desired.
>
> What resulted was a complete month-long vacation for a family that hadn't really taken a true break in over a decade. Family time, laughs, experiences, free time, adventure, and uninterrupted ponderings were to be had in abundance. We counted our blessings for such an opportunity and tried to make the most of it in our lives, resolving to spend more of our efforts on memories and less on materials. This meant simplification and a redoubled effort to make more of a difference in the lives of others.
>
> We also decided to wage a little war against electronic tyranny, implementing "black out" periods where we would occasionally, as a family, put ourselves beyond the reach of interruptions. The result of that one summer break in our lives has been profound. We learned together that sometimes you have to go slow in order to go fast.

"Memories rather than materials" is an excellent guideline for life.

Now Make It Real

Take some time right now and devise a written plan for implementing the "don't be normal" principles in this chapter. Put it into action and make it real. Also, do something in the next twenty-four hours that significantly adds to your memories.

Make this into a habit you never break.

NINETEEN

Ten Financial Danger Zones

I think the key indicator of wealth is not good grades, work ethic, or IQ. I believe it's relationships. Ask yourself two questions: How many people do I know, and how much ransom money could I get for each one?
—JAROD KINTZ, COMEDIAN

There are some financial problems you need to beware of: the danger zones of personal finance. Specifically, there are ten things that are probably the most dangerous moments in someone's financial life. Whenever you get near any of these ten things, stop, think about it, disengage your emotions, and engage your logic because all of these are thin ice.

1. Taxes – Make sure you get a good tax adviser because the tax code can be pretty complicated. Never break the law. Never skate the edge. But make sure you understand the tax laws so you don't waste a bunch of money that you're not required to pay.
2. Home Ownership – We have been taught that homes are great to own. Maybe that is true for some people in the right circumstances, but being a homeowner is one of the most expensive things you will ever do. Not only is the upkeep a significant expense, but property taxes and insurance are also very costly. In societies with weak or struggling economies, increased property

taxes will be one way that cities, municipalities, and other local governments attempt to stay afloat.

And despite popular myths, homes do not always go up in value. This was the big idea that got popped during the last housing bubble. Many people have found themselves upside down on their homes, meaning they owe more than the home is now worth. This is a bad place to be.

It is not our advice to own a home, or to avoid owning a home, but rather to be very wise. Do not make the mistake of seeing your home as a major investment, and think through the financial ramifications before you buy.

3. Divorce – Don't divorce him! Don't divorce her! Work it out! If you don't, it is going to cost a lot of money. Of course, you need to do what is right for you and your family. Our point is simply that this can be a very dangerous financial move, so think it through from all angles. It might be the most expensive thing you ever do.

4. Credit Cards – Many people need to stay away from credit cards. We discussed this earlier in the book, several times in fact, but if you have not yet followed our advice, then (for crying out loud) put the plastic back in the wallet. Cut them up. Get rid of the things. Freeze them. Lock them up. Just stop using them.

   Credit cards are fine for people who have proven their ability to be disciplined with their finances. But for those with challenges in this regard, this warning is properly aimed.

5. Lawsuits – They are very expensive, and they can distract from your work, business, family, and other

important facets of life. If you are living the principles of financial fitness in this book, you will have the best and only real preparation for lawsuits: savings and financial discipline. Avoid lawsuits whenever possible, and never look at them as a way to gain something financially.

6. Uninsured Accidents and Sickness – Look, we know this is a tough world. But we have seen people cancel their health insurance because they "can't afford it," yet they have tons of credit card debt, a flat screen TV, recreational vehicles, fancy cars, boats, etc.

   Get yourself some insurance. Sell some stuff. Walk around in a barrel in you have to! Get insured, even if it is just major medical insurance that kicks in if you have a big emergency. Protect yourself and your finances. Too much insurance is a waste and too little is a risk. Avoid both extremes.

   It is wise for people to look into getting the following kinds of insurance: Home/rental, car, major medical, life, disability, long-term care, and identity theft protection. Also look into what insurance is needed for your kind of business. Protect your assets.

7. Status Living – Having to keep up with the Joneses (or the Zhangs, as they increasingly say in China) can really kill your financial fitness. If you haven't noticed, the Joneses are probably broke. Following their example is bad for your finances.

   Actually, to tell the truth, the Zhangs are spending only a little and saving a lot. Keeping up with the Zhangs, and not the Joneses, is a really good idea.

To repeat what we already said, stop buying things you don't need with money you don't have to impress people you don't even like.

8. College Education – We use the word "education" kind of lightly, depending on what college and where you go. College has become ridiculously expensive, partly because of all the scholarships given out, but mostly because of the ease with which kids can get government loans. This tends to drive the whole market price up. Be very careful that you get what you pay for.

Take some time to think it through before you plunk down all that hard-earned money on a college just for reputation. Turn on your analytical brain, and treat it like an investment. Either make sure you (or your kids) get trained in something that will really bring the return you want, or focus more on getting a great education and less on getting a degree.

To be clear, we think you should get a truly excellent education. This is one of the most important investments you will ever make. We just don't believe this happens in college as often or as well as many people expect it to. If you do choose college, be sure you get the education you really want—or go and find it elsewhere.

Note that the costs of college rise about 8% annually, while statistics show that the cost of a college education isn't a very good investment anymore. A large percentage of people never work in the field of their degree, but they leave school with thousands of dollars in student loans. Ironically, as schools focus increasingly on narrow job training instead of broad education, people are getting less in the way of education and also using their expensive degrees less after graduation.

For example, 85% of people who graduated from college in 2011 were unable to find a job and moved back in with their parents. Even more stayed away but still could not find good employment. It is increasingly common to find people with prestigious college degrees working in menial or fast food jobs.

Peter Thiel, the billionaire co-founder of PayPal, recently offered a number of $100,000 grants to students who were willing to drop out of college and start a business. Many top leaders are increasingly seeing college as a waste of time. As college becomes more expensive and less valuable, we expect to see more such alternatives that work for people better than college.

Again, if you do go to college, focus on your education—not the conveyor belt requirements of the system.

9. Addictions – Very often when we talk to people and they have some serious holes in their finances, we find out there is some type of addiction behind the scenes. Fight those off. Get professional help. Get treatment. As tragic as these things are personally and to the family, they are also just as bad financially. Clean up your life.

10. Investments – The rule on investing is "buyer beware." If those seeking your investment need your money, they do not qualify for it. If you don't retain 100% control of your money, you are going to lose a whole lot of it; we promise. We have learned this through sad experience. The best investments are found on the YOU, Inc. Investment Hierarchy discussed earlier.

About 95% of North Americans should not be in Kiyosaki's "I" quadrant, which is investors only. Most should be in the "B" (business owner) quadrant. Those who try to become investors too soon are usually trying to invest like millionaires while earning like the middle class. This is the opposite of the real goal, as discussed earlier: To earn like a millionaire and live like the middle class. Also, the professionals generally slaughter amateur investors.

BE VERY, VERY CAREFUL AS YOU MAKE DECISIONS ABOUT THE DANGER ZONES: TAXES, HOME OWNERSHIP, DIVORCE, CREDIT CARDS, LAWSUITS, INSURANCE, SEEKING STATUS, COLLEGE, ADDICTIONS, AND INVESTMENTS. GET GOOD ADVICE FROM YOUR FINANCIAL MENTORS, AND STUDY THINGS IN DETAIL BEFORE TAKING ACTION.

As you become financially fit, do your best to avoid the financial danger zones, and be extremely careful as you make decisions when they do present themselves.

TWENTY

What It Means to Deserve

Americans used to be "citizens." Now we are "consumers."
—VICKI ROBIN

We have already talked about the importance of not use consumer debt. In other words, never finance anything that depreciates (aside from your home).

This one piece of advice, if followed, would save most people a lot of grief and keep them much more financially fit. The problem is that far too often people want jet skis, boats, motorcycles, trailers, gaming electronics, entertainment systems, trips to Hawaii, pools, and other things that don't appreciate.

When they hear that they can't buy these things if they want to be financially fit, they respond, "But I've worked so hard. I deserve it."

This is a clear misunderstanding of what it means to deserve something. The truth is, if you deserved it you would have the cash for it.

In other words, if you earn the money for it, you deserve it. If not, then you don't. If you are using debt to buy it, then you haven't earned the cash for it yet— so you don't deserve it. You might deserve it next month or next year, but not right now.

> **Never finance anything that depreciates.**

Only buy things when you actually deserve them, which means that you have earned the money, are out of debt, have already paid yourself first, and have the cash in hand.

Throughout this book, whether we have been discussing financial basics, offense, or defense, we keep coming back to this central point: Those who spend beyond their means are financially unfit. To get in financial shape, you have to reframe the way you see the world and understand that the principles of financial fitness are the key to money success.

People who are financially successful have nearly all had to say "No" many, many times to various purchases. But now they drive nice cars, live in nice homes, and most importantly, live their life dream because they delayed their purchases until they had the cash.

If you want to be successful in your finances and achieve your life vision, follow their example. It is amazing what kinds of storms and challenges you can weather when you follow these principles.

The 2X Rule

Many realtors say that you can afford a home priced at three times your annual income. So, by their reasoning, if you make $50,000 a year, you could afford a home that costs up to $150,000. But the Woodward Rule, as we call it, is that some realtors really want you to spend more on a home than you should. For home purchases, we suggest the 2X Rule, meaning that if you make $50,000 a year, you shouldn't spend more than $100,000 for your home. If you are renting your home, your monthly rental costs should be no more than 25–35% of your net, take-home income.

"But, that would be too small," many people say. "We have a taste for the finer things."

The correct response to this is, "Great! So go earn more, and then you will be able to afford more. Right now, you should follow the 2X Rule."

Let's be clear about how compound interest and mortgages work. Because of how much thirty years of interest costs in addition to the principal, you pay around $500,000 for a $150,000 house, so you can't really afford it at $50,000 a year. Before you sign a home loan, before you even go very far toward purchasing a house, ask your lender to tell you how much it will cost once you have paid it all off—including all principal and interest. Then find out how much the insurance will be and add that to your amount. Also, don't forget to factor in all the closing costs, fees, inspections, taxes, and the like, not to mention the upkeep.

This will help you see if you can really afford it, and in many cases, people can only afford a certain home if they have no emergency fund, no other savings, and finance most of their living expenses using debt. That is *not* affording it; that is going broke and deeper into debt.

What you want is to live in a house that you can truly afford and that allows you to save a lot, build up your resources and your business, and create real wealth. Then, when you have the cash, you can sell the house and buy a bigger one.

IF YOU BUY A HOME, FOLLOW THE 2X RULE. FOR EXAMPLE, IF YOUR INCOME IS $50,000 PER YEAR, DO NOT BUY A HOME THAT COSTS MORE THAN $100,000. IF YOU WANT A BIGGER HOME, EARN MORE MONEY.

When Orrin and his wife Laurie had their first year of big earnings, they were living in a very modest 1,900-square-foot home.

It was perfect for their needs, and it allowed them to focus on building their pipeline. Once they had the cash, they upgraded.

They bought an 8,200-square-foot home and financed it for thirty years. They put down $300,000 cash and had cash reserves on the side to pay off the house if needed. But they wanted to keep a large savings, so they used a loan for the rest of the home.

They negotiated for the best interest rate they could find, and they asked how soon they could pay off the loan without a penalty. The answer was three years. Then, as they earned more money, they paid off the house quickly to avoid interest. At the three-year mark, they paid off the home and owned it free and clear.

Once they paid off the home, they used the roll-down method, not to pay off debts (because they didn't have any), but to build even more savings. With no debt payments, they lived on 25% of their income and put away the 75% following the guidelines of the YOU, Inc. Investment Hierarchy.

Even though they were living on 25% of their income, they had enough money to buy some of the "toys" they had denied themselves over the years. Indeed, if you have "toys," it should mean that you are financially fit, living on a small percentage of your income, and paying cash for them.

At this point, it is okay to say that you have worked hard and you deserve a few "toys." If you are not financially fit and you have a bunch of "toys," it means that you do not really deserve them and you are using your savings or debt on the wrong things.

IF YOU ARE NOT FINANCIALLY FIT AND YOU HAVE A BUNCH OF "TOYS," IT MEANS THAT YOU DO NOT REALLY DESERVE THEM AND YOU ARE USING YOUR SAVINGS OR DEBT ON THE WRONG THINGS. IF YOUR DEBTS ARE ALL PAID OFF, YOU ARE FOLLOWING THE SAVINGS GUIDELINES LISTED IN EARLIER PRINCIPLES, AND YOU HAVE THE CASH, YOU CAN BUY A FEW "TOYS" AND STILL BE FINANCIALLY FIT.

Make It So!

Decide how to best apply the principles from this chapter in your life, and add them to your written financial plan. Be realistic and follow through.

Summary of Part III—Defense

- The principles of financial defense include:

  > PRINCIPLE 25: Get rid of debt.

  > PRINCIPLE 26: If you aren't financially sound, don't get caught in the trap of using "business debt."

  > PRINCIPLE 27: Do not use credit cards to build your credit because this almost always leads people to more debt.

  > PRINCIPLE 28: Never use title pawning, "ninety-days-same-as-cash" loans, payday loans, rent-to-own plans, layaway debt, or similar schemes.

  > PRINCIPLE 29: See your car(s) as transportation, not status symbols. Save up and always pay cash for them.

  > PRINCIPLE 30: Debit cards are better than credit cards for many people, and cash is even better.

  > PRINCIPLE 31: Teach your children and youth the principles of financial fitness. Set the example for them. Mentoring them will help you as well as them.

  > PRINCIPLE 32: If you are not wealthy, do not get sucked in to using second mortgages.

  > PRINCIPLE 33: Use the roll-down method to pay off all credit card debts and then apply it to all other debts.

  > PRINCIPLE 34: Learn to be skeptical of advertising, media, and marketing.

  > PRINCIPLE 35: Accumulate slowly; build your inventory of resources and wisdom, not stuff.

- PRINCIPLE 36: Get right with God, apply true principles in all areas of life including finances, pursue your stewardship, serve others—and leave impressing others in God's hands.

- PRINCIPLE 37: Do not use consumer debt. Wise financing for business investment may be okay at times, but consumer debt is like a cancer. Cut it out!

- PRINCIPLE 38: Make memories part of your lifestyle, budget, and life plan. Start simple and add big memories, too.

- PRINCIPLE 39: Be very, very careful as you make decisions about the danger zones: taxes, home ownership, divorce, credit cards, lawsuits, insurance, seeking status, college, addictions, and investments. Get good advice from your financial mentors, and study things in detail before taking action.

- PRINCIPLE 40: If you buy a home, follow the 2X Rule. For example, if your income is $50,000 per year, do not buy a home that costs more than $100,000. If you want a bigger home, earn more money.

- PRINCIPLE 41: If you are not financially fit and you have a bunch of "toys," it means that you do not really deserve them and you are using your savings or debt on the wrong things. If your debts are all paid off, you are following the savings guidelines listed in earlier principles, and you have the cash, you can buy a few "toys" and still be financially fit.

PLAYING FIELD

"NOT IN OUR HOUSE!"

When an opposing team comes to play in your home
stadium, your teammates will frequently say, "Not in
our house!" This means that on your home turf, you
have a home-field advantage, but this only works if
your team knows the rules and understands the special
characteristics of the playing field. In Part IV, we will
discuss the overarching principles of financial fitness
and the economics that directly impact financial and life
choices. Knowing the economic playing field is essential
for financial success.

I don't understand technology, so I don't invest in it.
—WARREN BUFFETT

Wall Street predicted nine out of the last five recessions!
—PAUL SAMUELSON

TWENTY-ONE

The First Three Great Economic Questions

The businessman's tool is values;
the bureaucrat's tool is fear.
—AYN RAND

Imagine a group of people who are stranded on an island with no hope of ever being rescued or getting off the island. At first, the focus is all about survival, but soon the people realize the need for a more lasting solution to the daily process of meeting their various needs.

As a result, the people on the island do what societies always do: Ask the first five great economic questions. In this chapter, we will learn about the first three of these questions, and then we will cover the other two in later chapters.

The process of answering these questions in a society sometimes happens formally, but usually it just occurs naturally as the people experience needs and seek solutions. One way or another, all five questions are asked and answered in every society.

Together these basic questions make up what is known as macroeconomics, the large, society-level issues of economic life. The answers to the five big questions determine the character of each society, nation, and its people. In contrast, microeconomics deals with the choices made by an individual or a business for him-, her-, or itself.

In this book so far, we have been covering microeconomics, but as you get that under control, it will be more and more necessary for you to understand the overall environment in which your personal microeconomy operates.

Understanding these questions (and their answers) is an important part of becoming financially fit because successful people understand the playing field in which they live, work, play, earn, serve, and pursue happiness. This is vital information. No matter how strong your offense or defense, and no matter how good you are at the basics, if you do not understand the rules and the layout of the playing field, your team is going to lose.

For example, the first five great economic questions explain the difference between modern Hong Kong and Cuba. Those who don't understand these questions of free enterprise won't deeply understand the principles of financial fitness.

**STUDYING AND UNDERSTANDING FREE ENTERPRISE
IS AN ESSENTIAL PART OF FINANCIAL FITNESS.**

Question #1: How Will People Get the Necessities of Life?

The first big question of our island society, and of every society, is simple: How will the people get the necessities of life? In some places and time periods through history, this question has been asked by leaders, at other times by a family or an individual, and at different times by tribes, communities, nations, cities, towns, and other groups. But it is the first obvious economic question that every individual must answer even if there is no group.

There are four potential answers to the first great question. *One* is that people will just have to figure out how to survive on their own and fend entirely for themselves. Under this arrangement, they won't work together, so they don't really partake of an economy but simply live in isolation. The great political thinkers of history (such as Hume, Rousseau, and Locke) called this "The State of Nature," meaning a person or family living alone outside of society and without engaging in economic trade.

Such primitive economies are naturally high on freedom and low on prosperity and advancement, as long as the isolated individual or family stays safe. Usually, however, such a situation is very unsafe (because of stronger attackers and bandits), and the people in it experience low security as well as low prosperity. Simple survival becomes the name of the game.

A *second* possible answer to the question of how people will meet their physical needs is to work out most of their survival on their own, but interact with others through trade and economic exchange. This creates a barter economy in which people trade their goods and services for the products and services of others. Trade in barter economies works as long as both parties to a trade value what they are getting more than what they are giving.

Barter economies are usually high in freedom and fairly low in prosperity, mainly because most of the people spend the majority of their time just seeking the basics of life like water, fire, food, and shelter. They barter goods that help with these fundamental needs, and once in a while, they trade other things like shiny metal jewelry or the services of religion, technological advances, or art.

But without specialization (where some people focus their time on getting food and then trade the excess with those who become proficient in making clothes or shoes or building better shelters, etc.), barter societies seldom create widespread wealth, leisure, or advanced products and services.

Command vs. Market Economies

The *third* answer to the question of how people will meet their basic needs is to have a few people run things, rule over the others, and tell them what to do with their time and how to distribute their labor and belongings. This is called command economics, and it has been used more often than any other system over the course of human history. Unfortunately, command economies are always based on force and maintained with violence.

In command economies, freedom is low and prosperity is also low—except for the few who are in charge. The ruling class often uses its power to amass great wealth for itself, and as a result, command economies can become very advanced and attain high levels of technology and growth. Still, such advances are nearly always used to benefit the power of those in charge and keep the masses under their control.

A *fourth* possible answer to the question of how people will get the necessities of life is for everyone to agree on a few important and mutually beneficial rules and otherwise fend for himself or herself. This adoption of a few key rules changes everything, however. This system, called free enterprise, may seem a lot like a barter economy, but in fact, it is very different.

Property Rights

Specifically, in barter economies, people have no way to store their wealth and the fruits of their labor. If they try, they find that there are no rules to stop others from simply taking their stuff. Indeed, it is normal in pure barter societies for the strong to offer the following trade to those who are weaker: "Give us the food you stored up for winter, or we'll take your life."

There is no rule, law, or strong authority to stop this kind of plunder, so in barter societies those who save or invest are usually wasting their efforts.

When the people agree on a few simple rules of property and rights, however, this changes. They are able to store the fruits of their labor, and as a result, savings, investment, and advanced products, services, and technology naturally occur.

Free-enterprise economies only work when the rules treat everyone in the society the same and protect each person's life, liberty, and property from others. This is the basis of all free societies, and through history, it has been known simply as "the rights of property."

These rights are also sometimes referred to as "inalienable rights," the phrase used in the Declaration of Independence. Indeed, the American founders affirmed that the entire purpose of government is to protect these basic rights and that if a government stops doing this, it has outlived its purpose and should be abolished and replaced.

> **People living in free-enterprise economies experience higher levels of freedom and prosperity.**

This first great question of society is clearly very important. People living in free-enterprise economies experience higher levels of freedom and prosperity, making this the best of the four possible answers to the first great economic question.

Specialization

Another important thing happens when a society chooses a free-enterprise economy. Because people can safely save the fruits of their work, they are able to specialize and become experts at one skill or service or at creating one product—and then trade their excess for the work of other specialists. This leads to advanced economies and significant growth, prosperity, and power.

Note that such advances come whenever savings and assets are protected, either by the rules of free-enterprise societies or the power of rulers in command economies. Thus, command and free-enterprise cultures build complex societies, while individuals trying to survive outside society and groups relying on barter remain at relatively simple levels.

Question #2: Who Will Rule?

When a group adopts a command or free-enterprise economy, this immediately brings up the second great economic question: Who will be in charge of making and enforcing the rules?

In command economies, the answer is that the rulers are in charge of everything. Sometimes this means a king, emperor, caesar, tsar, or dictator rules, and other societies adopt a whole class of rulers called aristocrats, ruling upper classes, or elites.

In free-enterprise societies, in contrast, the rulers are the people themselves, either personally (in very small societies) or through representatives (in bigger nations). There are many different arrangements of this system, but the best of them in history have given only limited powers to the government and then created checks and balances to keep governments from turning into command economies.

This is one of the repeating patterns of history: Every government eventually seeks to increase its power, and the rulers in every economic arrangement eventually try to move toward a command economy—with themselves in charge.

> This is one of the repeating patterns of history: Every government eventually seeks to increase its power.

When the people oversee government and keep it in line, the government does two main things: 1) It protects the inalienable rights of its people against foreign attack, and 2) It protects the life, liberty, and property of the citizens against internal attack. Free government and true free enterprise only exist when government does these two things and leaves *everything* else to the people themselves. As Thomas Jefferson taught, a nation governs best that governs least.

This is the basis of freedom in all nations everywhere and at all times throughout history. To the extent that nations have followed this model, they have been free—and the opportunity for prosperity has been widespread.

Note that the first great question (how will people get the necessities of life?) is the foundation of economics, and the second (who will rule?) is the basis of government. Thus, economics is naturally primary, and politics is secondary.

Question #3: How Will the People Keep the Government in Check?

As we mentioned earlier, all governments, even those established in free-enterprise societies, naturally try to adopt command economies and increase the force, control, and wealth of the rulers. As a response, the third great question is: How will the people keep the government in check? How can they keep it focused on protecting freedom and prevent it from turning the society into a command economy?

The answer, whatever it is in a specific society, becomes the constitution of the nation. A constitution is a set of rules given by the people to keep the government under control. In contrast, laws are rules given by governments to the people.

Constitutions are therefore superior to laws, and all laws in truly free nations must adhere to the constitution. If not, the society is on a sure path to becoming a force-based command economy—be-

> **Constitutions are superior to laws, and all laws in truly free nations must adhere to the constitution.**

cause the laws will naturally benefit the economic needs and wants of the ruling class, while a good constitution protects the life, liberty, and property of everyone.

> **When free enterprise declines, the obstacles to financial fitness always increase.**

Free enterprise flourishes in nations with good constitutions, as long as the people keep the government in line. When free enterprise declines, the obstacles to financial fitness always increase.

As a result, those who want to remain financially fit closely study the principles of economics, government, and freedom as well as the rules of financial fitness.

FINANCIALLY FIT PEOPLE WHO WANT TO MAINTAIN AN ENVIRONMENT THAT ENCOURAGES OPPORTUNITY AND PROSPERITY PAY ATTENTION TO THE PRINCIPLES OF FREEDOM AND THE ONGOING ACTIONS OF GOVERNMENT.

Action

Make a study of freedom and free enterprise part of your long-term personal plan. This is an important part of investing in yourself and in the future. Get started right away!

TWENTY-TWO

The Fourth Great Economic Question: Is the Economy as Good as Gold?

It's a recession when your neighbor loses his job; it's a depression when you lose your own.
—HARRY S. TRUMAN

The first three great economic questions establish whether a nation will be based on freedom or force, who will be in charge, and how those in charge will be kept from abusing their power. These are very important foundations of any society. In fact, all of them are ultimately economic questions because they deal with how to get the necessities of life and how to protect life, liberty, and property.

Question #4: What Will Be Used as Currency?

Once a society has determined that it will adopt free enterprise and maintain it with a free government system, and once it has also established effective ways to keep the government from switching to a command economy and stealing the peoples' property and assets, a fourth great question arises: What will be used as currency?

This choice has a drastic, lasting influence on a nation's success and on the individual financial fitness of its citizenry. The fourth great economic question is as important as the first three, but few people understand how essential it is—because most people don't quite "get" how money really works.

Good Currency

At its core, currency is a store of wealth. It is a store (or savings) of a person's hard work, risk, and effort. Good currency is also much easier to trade than the actual fruits of one's labor. For example, a farmer who tries to store eggs and trade them for clothes months later will find that they spoil and lose their value before he can spend them. If he can sell them today, however, and save the good currency he gets for them, the currency will still be valuable six months from now when he wants to purchase clothes for his family.

This simple example is duplicated in millions of different ways, every month by people from all walks of life, and a good currency allows them to store their wealth and use it when they actually need it. It allows them to pay themselves first, save for emergencies, save up for big purchases, and invest in themselves and in business. Again, if they try to do these things with apples or milk, the fruits of their labor will be lost.

As a result, societies with good currencies waste far less of their prosperity (they sell the eggs before they spoil) and increase in affluence much more quickly than nations without an advantageous currency.

There are several important characteristics of good currency:

1. It stores wealth effectively and lasts a long time (longevity).
2. It is easily divisible so people can use it to purchase things of various prices (divisibility).
3. It is simple to measure (measurability).
4. It is easy to transport (transportability).

5.   It maintains a stable value (stability).

6.   It keeps governments and national banks from spending more than they have (untamperability).

Most economic textbooks only teach the first four characteristics of good money, but the last two are essential. Indeed, if anything, maintaining a stable value of money and keeping the government honest are even more important than divisibility, longevity, measurability, and transportability. And through history, gold is the only currency that has proven able to accomplish all of these important traits.

Types of Currency

There are several kinds of currency. One is commodity money, which means that it has value of its own because it is something people want. As we already said, to be useful, commodity money has to be easily measurable, easily divisible, and it needs to last. Thus eggs and carrots, though they have intrinsic value, would not be good stores of value. Wheat and corn last a little longer than eggs and carrots, but not long enough to be good currency. And carrying barrels of wheat around is a bit cumbersome.

Precious metals have become the standard of commodity money. Because they are rare, people want them, and they meet the other requirements such as divisibility, measurability, and longevity. They have proven to be a good store of wealth because their value remains stable over time. Indeed, the gold standard (with silver for smaller coins and purchases) has been the only stable currency throughout history.

> **Gold is the only currency that has proven able to accomplish all of the important traits of good money.**

A second kind of money is metal-backed money, meaning that you get a paper bill or a check or certificate, and you can trade it in for gold or silver whenever you want. This makes it easy for people to transport large sums when they travel.

Another type of money is fiat money, which is used as currency only because a government says so (by dictate or "fiat"). Fiat money is not backed by any precious metal or commodity and is only accepted by other people as long as they believe it can be used to buy real goods and services. Through history, there have been numerous losses of wealth when people traded their products or work for fiat money and then discovered that others refused to accept it as currency.

In fact, very often, governments print fiat money on purpose because they want to spend more than the allotted funds they have available. So they just print on some paper, add their stamp of approval, and spend it. When this happens, they are able to buy things at today's prices, but as soon as they do this, the money inflates.

Inflation

Inflation means that the currency is less scarce so, from now on, people will require more of it for purchases. In other words, there is more currency in circulation trying to buy the same amount of goods. As a result, prices rise, and things cost more. At the same time, salaries and contracts usually remain the same, so most people get the same amount of income but find that they can't buy nearly as much with it as they could before.

If individuals printed a value on a piece of paper and bought things with it (while the people who accepted it could not buy anything with it, or could only buy less), they would be arrested for counterfeiting and fraud. This is precisely what happens when people write bad checks. But this is exactly what most governments do, and it has caused numerous recessions and economic depressions throughout history.

The framers of the U.S. Constitution made it unconstitutional for the U.S. government to use fiat money. (They required all currency to be in gold and silver.) But the government has found ways to break this principle for almost the last century of American history. Today most modern governments print fiat money, and the United States is unfortunately one of the leaders in this practice.

The Middle-Class Squeeze

This choice by government to inflate the currency is especially hard on the middle class, which tends to keep its savings (if any) in cash or the bank. The wealthy, in contrast, keep a little currency on hand but put most of their savings into other things— gold, silver, precious jewels, land, real estate, business ownership, investments, and so on.

When the government inflates the currency so it can spend more, these non-cash assets of the wealthy do not lose their value, but the money the middle class has in the bank isn't worth nearly as much as before.

IN ADDITION TO CASH SAVINGS, SAVE SOME OF YOUR MONEY IN SOMETHING OTHER THAN FIAT CURRENCY.

When governments use fiat money, the divide between the rich and the middle classes consistently grows. Under such circumstances, it becomes more challenging for those in the middle classes to pay their bills, while the rich naturally get richer. This is the system we follow today, but most people do not realize what is going on.

In fact, the Soviet leader Vladimir Lenin once said, "The best way to destroy the capitalist system is to debauch the currency." Debauch literally means to debase, which comes from the ancient practice of mixing lesser metals into more precious metals. Lenin's reasoning was that this strategy would successfully get rid of the prosperity of the middle class in a way that hardly any of the regular people would know what happened. Sadly, this has proven far too true.

A good, stable metal currency does not allow this to happen. Indeed, one way to tell if a politician really supports the needs of the middle class is how strongly he or she supports the end of fiat currency and the adoption or maintenance of the gold standard. Of course, this alone is not the only measure of an elected official's sincerity, but it is one clear indication of whether the focus is on helping the middle class, and of whether he or she understands how things works.

As we mentioned, almost nobody really understands the power of currency. If more people knew how important this is, more modern nations would adopt the gold standard (assuming the people were given any choice in the matter).

Today, nearly all nations use fiat money. Because of this, it is important to learn more about the history of gold and the need for metal and metal-backed currency in the modern world. We will do more of this in the next chapter.

TWENTY-THREE

The Financial Matrix and a Brief History of Gold

Whoever does not wish to render history incomprehensible by departmentalizing it—political, economic, social—would perhaps take the view that it is in essence a battle of dominant wills, fighting in every way they can for the material which is common to everything they construct: the human labor force.
—BERTRAND DE JOUVENEL

The Law of the Increase of Production Depends on those of Three Elements—Labor, Capital, and Land.
—JOHN STUART MILL

The Financial Matrix?

Bertrand de Jouvenel, the French political philosopher, in his book *On Power*, wrote one of the most profound thoughts (quoted above) on humanity and history. To summarize, Jouvenel stated that history is the record of how the dominant wills (the aristocracy) capture control of the productive capacity of the masses. By combining this statement with John Stuart Mill's statement above on the three classical factors of production (labor, land, and capital), one is in a position to test Jouvenel's theory. For if history is truly the record of aristocrats capturing the masses' production, then they must do so by capturing either the labor, land, or capital, since these are the only three factors of production. In chapter five of his GUINNESS WORLD RE-CORDS® official record–setting book *And Justice For All*, Orrin revealed the three types of exploitation throughout history, with today's Financial Matrix being just the latest variety of control.

1. Physical Matrix (Slavery): Control human beings to control the labor.
2. Land Matrix (Serfdom): Control the land to indirectly control the labor.
3. Financial Matrix (Subjugation): Control the capital to indirectly control the labor.

Orrin identified the Five Laws of Decline (FLD) to describe how the elites have controlled the masses historically. He wrote:

The FLD exploitation of the masses' production by elites originated with the elites controlling the masses' labor (physical slavery) to control production. Indeed, for thousands of years, this was the preferred method of control. Over time, however, this method fell out of favor as Christianity permeated Roman society. As it became increasingly intolerable for Christians to enslave fellow Christians (regrettably, enslaving non-Christians was still tolerable), the exploiters switched to the second factor of production, land. Instead of physical slavery, the masses now endured land serfdom, as the elites owned and controlled the land. The elites' direct ownership of the land gave them indirect ownership of the people. Fortunately for the people, however, as the free-market system blossomed, they were no longer beholden to the land-owning aristocracy for survival and were increasingly able to prosper through private enterprise and businesses of their own.

It is not hard to guess what the elites did next, given that there was only one input of production (capital) left to control. As predicted, when feudalism had run its course and private enterprise began to spread, the battle between state and society for the control of capital commenced. Although society at first successfully created a gold standard (which checked the state's ability to control the monetary system), the elite statists eventually regained the upper hand. The state (always hungry for funds to increase its power) finally wrestled money away from the FLD-restraining gold standard and became capital's sole creator, owner, and controller. They did this through the artifices of the central banking system's centralized planning of the money supply. By directly controlling the monetary system, the elites indirectly control the masses' production, since nearly everyone uses capital (the third input of all production) in today's money economies. The exploitation of capital by the elites confirms in practice what a study of the FLD and its interaction with the three factors of production predicted in theory.

This is why there is so much talk about returning to the gold standard, as the gold standard prevents the state from manipulating the money supply for its benefit to the detriment of its citizens.

The Gold Standard

Low taxes, stable money. Could it really be so simple? The idea that lower taxes could lead to a healthier, more vibrant

> *economy—and healthier, more vibrant government*
> *finances—is timeless and arguably self-evident.*
> —NATHAN LEWIS

Some people believe gold was designed by God specifically to be used as money. Whether or not this is true, gold has a lot going for it. Gold is malleable, imperishable, chemically inert, and extremely dense. It can be pounded into sheets as thin as five millionths of an inch, and one ounce of gold can be pulled out as a wire fifty miles long. An ounce of gold can also be pounded into 100 square feet.

In short, it's pretty cool. There are stories of refugees pounding out gold around their body in order to escape with wealth, and most of the Earth's gold that has ever been mined is still around. All the available gold could be melted down to a block 60 x 60 x 60 feet in size, a cube that would weigh 125 to 135 thousand tons! This block could easily fit on a single cargo ship. All of this shows how rare gold is.

Human history is full of obsessions with gold and warnings about it. For example, in the fifth century, Pindar called gold a child of Zeus. He noted that neither moth nor rust devoirs it, but that it too frequently devours and controls the mind of man.

John Ruskin told the story of a man who had a bag of gold on a ship during a storm. He had to jump off the ship to swim to shore for safety, but he never arrived because he was trying to hang on to his heavy bag of treasure. The moral of the story is clear: Did the man own a bag of gold, or did the gold actually own him?

Other Currencies

Gold has been determined to be the best currency by nearly every civilization in history, and it has been highly valued for thousands of years. Author Addison Wiggin wrote:

Even people who are worlds apart in some ways can still agree in others. What did Karl Marx and Andrew Carnegie agree on? That gold is the only worthwhile money....

"Throughout history, many types of currency...were rejected in favor of gold: cowrie shells, cows, wheat, giant stone disks, strings of beads, cauldrons and iron tripods, metal rings, copper, bronze, silver, and even cocoa beans and whales' teeth."[17]

None of these lasted.

Over the years, many people and governments have tried to manipulate gold by mixing it with other metals, but any merchant with a scale easily detects this. Because of this trait, gold and silver have the special ability to keep governments, banks, and other users honest in their financial dealings.

As historian Nathan Lewis put it: "The world's commercial centers have used one or another variant of gold for most of the last three millennia. And for good reason: gold forces governments to be fiscally responsible [because even governments can't make fiat gold] and it provides a stable environment for rapid economic growth as well as a safe environment for individual investors to grow their own wealth."[18]

Paper Money

So if gold is such a great currency, how did the world get away from using it? It all began when paper money was invented to make it easier to transport wealth. Goldsmiths kept gold for people and gave them receipts to verify how much they had on deposit. Then the people could travel to another city or country and use the receipt without having to carry large trunks of gold in their wagons or ships. Eventually, people simply started trading the receipts themselves for goods and services.

Some sneaky goldsmiths even began issuing more receipts than they had gold, which allowed them to spend more than they actually had. They were able to get away with this as long as everyone did not demand their gold all at once. This led to something called *fractional-reserve banking*, a system in which banks loan out more money than they actually have on hand.

Today, this is legal and commonplace in most nations. But at times of great economic difficulty, there have been runs on the banks where everyone tried to withdraw their cash at the same time, and the banks were forced to close down. Governments have even decreed "bank holidays," which means they close the bank for a time to hopefully wait out the panic and to stop such runs on the banks. In many cases, these banks never reopened and people simply lost their savings.

Way back in the eighth century, leaders in China began issuing pure fiat money, paper currency that could not be traded in for gold or silver. This money looked like gold receipts, and people took it because the government vouched for its value and forced them to accept it.

Again, governments often get away with this because the middle class doesn't understand what is happening, and the upper classes do not stop it because they store most of their money in non-fiat assets. As we said before, this is one major way the ruling classes get richer.

So over time, the world drifted from the sound money of gold to the inflatable money of fiat paper.

How Inflation Works

The concepts of fiat money and inflation can be difficult to grasp. Think of it this way. Imagine you are at a fundraising auction for cakes with your local scouts or church youth group. Everyone is bidding on cakes, and some people pay up to $20 or $30 for a cake. It's for a good cause, so you join the bidding. You know you can get a cake from Walmart or even the bakery for a lot less. But your kids are looking at you to see if you are one of the cool parents, so you get into the spirit of things and bid on a cake or two.

Then someone walks through the room and hands each person $150 in $10 bills. You look at your newfound stack of bills totaling $150, and you look around the room and see everyone else is getting the same amount. "Awesome!" you tell yourself.

Your first thought is to stick the new money into your wallet and put it toward your $1,000 savings fund, right? But suddenly the next cake goes up for auction. What do you think happens to the auction? Where the price of cakes averaged $12 to $18 before, things are different now. Everyone just got $150 in $10 bills! So what do they do?

You know what comes next. Someone bids $30 on the cake, another dad ups it to $50, and pretty soon, you can't get a cake for less than a hundred bucks.

That's how inflation works. The big difference is that in the auction, someone just *handed* you the money, but in real life, the government borrowed it from China—and only handed it out to *some* of the people. Or, they "printed" the new money and made it available to a small circle of bankers who are in on the game with them.

Oh, and next Thursday, you will get a tax bill in the mail to cover what was "redistributed." But since the government is paying interest on the money it handed out, and since some of the people do not owe taxes for a number of reasons, your bill is actually $187 instead of the $150 you received at the auction. Plus, you already spent the money on a cake! (Actually, since you are applying all the principles of financial fitness covered in this book, you saved $15 [paying yourself 10% first!], paid $15 toward your debts, and put $15 toward your fund for a new car. So you ended up getting a $105 cake.)

The same thing happens in real life. When the government prints more money, that does not suddenly mean there are more products on the shelves of stores. There is more money, but the same number of things to buy. Thus there is less demand for the money (because there is a lot more of it now), but the same demand for the items in the store—so the price of the things naturally goes up. This is inflation.

Is It Stealing?

Let's be clear: Inflation stinks! And the major cause of inflation is governments printing or producing more fiat money. When they do this, just like they did with the fictional cake auction, merchants soon realize that there is more currency in the economy and prices go up. This is happening right now—today, and tonight while you sleep. There is an old saying that interest never sleeps, and it doesn't. Neither does inflation.

That is why the gold standard is very important. Nations using the gold standard do not use fiat currency, and as a result, inflation is very small or nonexistent because a government cannot simply produce more of it. That is how you want your nation to do it.

As we have discussed the principles of financial fitness in this book, we have talked a lot about not wasting your money on unnecessary purchases, resisting shopaholism even when you can afford something, avoiding all consumer debt, and being disciplined in your saving. But the government is still taking some of your hard-earned money every time it produces fiat currency. Then it sends you a tax bill to cover the cost of inflating your money.

As long as the majority of people stand for it, this practice will continue. Frederic Bastiat called this kind of government behavior "legal plunder." It is legal because the government makes the laws, but it is still a form of stealing.

Solutions

Of course, the big solution to this kind of plunder is to convince the government to stop using fiat money and implement the gold standard. If this doesn't happen, keep trying, and keep telling people about it. Have them read this book so they will realize just what a big deal this is.

If enough people support this change, the government in your nation will eventually have to give in. In the meantime, there are ways to wisely use commodities to store your savings more safely.

Always keep some cash and some savings in the bank. Refer to the YOU, Inc. Investment Hierarchy discussed earlier. And at some point, consider investing in gold and silver.

You probably get paid for your job or business in paper, fiat money. Putting some of that fruit of your labor into precious metal will make it easier to keep your savings during economic downturns, and even just protect it from the normal rate of inflation.

The United States went off the gold standard in 1933, and many economists believe that this had a direct impact on worsening the Great Depression. At that point, foreign banks could still trade U.S. currency for gold, but American citizens could not. In fact, it was illegal to own gold (except jewelry and old coins for collecting), and for several years, people were required to turn in their gold in exchange for fiat currency. Then in 1971, the United States stopped giving *anyone* gold in exchange for its currency. This remains U.S. law today, though people can now own gold.

In comparison, China made owning gold legal in 2004, and in 2011 the Hong Kong Mercantile Exchange began trading silver. In 2012, many Chinese investors stopped buying U.S. dollars and started increasing their investments in gold. China is the world's largest producer of gold, and it is now the world's second largest importer of gold. In contrast, back in 1980, 15% of Americans owned silver, compared with less than 1% today. Far less than 1% of Americans now have gold savings.[19]

Warnings

Note that it is usually bad to put money into gold if you have not invested in yourself first. Invest in your knowledge, leadership, financial fitness, personal development, and in your career and business before you start putting away storage in metals.

STUDY UP ON INVESTMENTS IN METAL, AND ANY OTHER INVESTMENT, BEFORE YOU BUY. DO YOUR HOMEWORK. TAKE YOUR TIME.

Don't count on your metal money to go up a lot in value. It will usually just be pretty stable. If it goes up for a while, do not get speculative. You put your cash into metal to store it and save it more safely, not to get a big return on it. But fiat money will certainly lose value, so having more stable savings in gold or silver is helpful.

Investing in metals is analogous to freezing fruit. The fruit of our labors, if in the form of fiat money, will perish through inflation. "Freeze" this fruit to preserve it whole by converting it to precious metals. But just as no one expects their frozen fruit to multiply, your precious metals should not really be expected to go up in value either. They merely serve to "freeze" the fruits of your labor.

> **Investing in metals is analogous to freezing fruit.**

For example, the U.S. dollar has lost 96% of its purchasing power since the year 1913. That is mostly because of the govern-

234

ment printing fiat currency. In contrast, an ounce of gold in 1913 and today would buy about the same things. So when it appears that gold is going up in value, as measured in U.S. dollars, for instance, it is really just indicating how much the currency has been inflated.

As we said earlier, do not invest in things you don't know about, or you will probably make a lot of mistakes and lose money. If and when you want to put some of your cash savings into metals, do your homework first.

Sometimes when you buy gold, part of the cost goes to the value of the coins for collectors. When you buy bullion, in contrast, you are paying for only the value of the metal. But many nations, including the United States, allow the government to confiscate gold bullion in times of national crisis. There are a number of nuances like this, so do not buy until you educate yourself.

There are also a lot of scams and shysters and just bad advice surrounding gold and silver investments. There are trustworthy companies too, so do your research. The overarching principle is to get the most metal for the least amount of money. Again, like with any investments, really study the topic in detail so you don't get burned.

Do not get too caught up in this, but educate yourself about metals and use them to help protect your savings. Don't be like Crassus in ancient Rome who was a money-hungry tyrant. One account of his death says his enemies who poured molten gold down his throat. Instead of being swayed by gold or riches of any kind, focus on financial fitness and let the principles naturally increase your prosperity.

Above all, as we have said several times already, focus on using the blessings God gives you for His glory! Your stewardship is what really matters, so use it wisely.

Make It Happen

Learn ways to apply what you have learned in this chapter and take action. Be wise as you research where to store your money beyond cash savings. Make a plan to study investment in metals. Really know what you are doing before you ever buy, and discuss your plans with your mentor.

TWENTY-FOUR

The Fifth Great Economic Question: What Is Your Enterprise?

No enterprise can exist for itself alone. It ministers to some great need, it performs some great service, not for itself, but for others; failing therein, it ceases to be profitable and ceases to exist.
—CALVIN COOLIDGE

We have already covered the first four great economic questions that form any society's rules and its playing field for financial success. Knowing these rules and the contours of the playing field is essential to getting financially fit. To summarize, the first four questions are:

1. How will people get the necessities of life?
2. Who will be in charge of making and enforcing the rules? (Who will rule?)
3. How will the people keep the rulers from stealing the fruits of their labor? (How will the people keep the government in check?)
4. What will be used as currency?

Freedom and prosperity flourish when societies respond to these questions by adopting the following: a free-enterprise economic system, rule by the people themselves rather than any elite governing group, strong but limited free government that follows a good constitution, and a stable currency.

How to Flourish

Even if your nation has not adopted all of these things, you can still be financially fit by following the principles outlined in this book, but it will be more difficult. As we have said before, "The more people ignore economics, the more their money and wealth will be taken, and the harder life will be."[20]

Over time, nations either move in the direction of "less free and less prosperous" or "more free and more prosperous." Part of long-term financial fitness is using your influence to help your nation move in the right direction.

If your society has adopted all of these positive things (free enterprise, free government, a good constitution that keeps the government in line, and the gold standard), you will see it greatly increase in strength and wealth. Applying the principles of financial fitness will be easier, and the returns will naturally be greater.

Question #5: What Will Be Your Enterprise?

Either way, this fifth question is vital, and only you can really answer it. The good news is that you have true control over your response to the fifth great economic question:

5. What will your great enterprise be right now and immediately ahead?

This question is at the heart of greatness, individually and nationally. What will your enterprise be? We already discussed this in the chapter on choosing your business, but on the large scale, a society of people choosing enterprise is one of the most important issues of macroeconomics. Some societies are enterprising, and therefore free and widely prosperous, while others are not.

Enterprise is a profound word. It comes from the fifteenth-century French word *entreprende,* which carried the direct meaning of "to undertake" and also the more general significance of "a spirit of daring." The dictionary lists the following synonyms to the word enterprise: enterprising, mastermind, entrepreneur, venture, private, and free.[21] *The Oxford English Thesaurus* adds the following synonyms as well: business, initiative, resourcefulness, enthusiasm, dynamism, boldness, courageous, and adventurous.

This fifth great question is asked by every society and nation, as well as by each business, family, and individual. What will we stand for? What will we be known for? Who are we? How will we spend our lives? What is our enterprise?

When nations ask this, it is the last of the five great macroeconomic questions. When businesses, families, and individuals ask the same thing, it is the beginning of microeconomics, as discussed earlier. Thus, it is a vital question for both fields.

As we have said before:

> How is wealth created? How is wealth maintained? How do people trade resources? Most people view these things as mysterious or some kind of…magic. Or they think these kinds of questions don't really matter. But they are very important. They determine your freedom and your lifestyle. Economics boils down to choices and ultimately who will make the choices—you or the government?
>
> History shows the truth of what works and what doesn't work. There is no bureaucrat or government agency that can make hundreds of millions of choices as well as the regular people can make them.[22]

Moreover, there is no government that can make your choices for you better than you can.

INVEST EVEN MORE IN YOURSELF BY LEARNING TO BE THE KIND OF PERSON WHO CONSISTENTLY ENGAGES IN AN ENTERPRISING, CREATIVE, ENTHUSIASTIC TYPE OF LIFE. FILL YOUR DAYS WITH ENTERPRISE, ACTION, AND DOING THINGS THAT MATTER. AND TEACH YOUR CHILDREN AND THE PEOPLE YOU WORK WITH TO DO THE SAME. BECOME THE KIND OF PERSON AND LEADER WHO CONSISTENTLY WORKS ON YOUR CURRENT ENTERPRISE.

As more people take the enterprising approach to life, whole societies are hugely influenced for good. The collective, individually chosen enterprise of a nation of free people is one of the most powerful forces in all human history.

Invest in yourself by learning to be the kind of person who consistently engages in an enterprising, creative, enthusiastic type of life. Fill your days with enterprise, action, and doing things that matter. And teach your children and the people you work with to do the same.

> **The collective, individually chosen enterprise of a nation of free people is one of the most powerful forces in all human history.**

Free enterprise declines when the people become complacent or apathetic, leave things to others or the government, and/or just go to work, watch TV, and go to bed. Become the kind of person and leader who consistently works on your current enterprise. As you do this, and as you help others to do the same, you will have a long-term influence for good.

TWENTY-FIVE

The Camel in the Tent

A penny saved is a government oversight.
—CHRIS BRADY

Take honest stock of your national economy (and the world economy), and prepare accordingly. The years ahead may bring small economic ups and downs, like the ones that normally happen to any economy over time. Or they may bring medium-sized shocks, like the Great Recession of 2008–2013, where most of the economy suffers but some sectors and businesses still grow.

They may even bring a major downturn, like the Great Depression or the huge crash that happened in the 1860s, where almost everyone is hurt and the economy grows stagnant for a long period of time. Indeed, the economy runs in cycles, and unfortunately, another major economic challenge may be due sometime in the next decade.[23] Whatever comes, those who have prepared for such events will be ready and able to help others if things get bad (and even if they don't).

Over the years many economists have attempted to predict the coming ups and downs of the economy, but this has proven to be a very tricky business. Weather forecasting is more accurate than most economic predictions, so it is important to be prepared for anything. That said, part of being financially fit is studying economics and paying attention to what is happening in the world.

Austrian Economics

As inaccurate as most economic forecasts tend to be, there is one group of economic thinkers that has consistently provided the best economic commentary and advice. The Austrian school of economics, as it is called, is the oldest, most consistent, and best at predicting the economic cycle. The most well-known authors of the Austrian school include Friedrich Hayek, Ludwig von Mises, and Murray Rothbard.

While most economists focus on mathematical models and use technical language beyond the understanding of many regular people, the Austrian economists teach economics in a different way. According to the Austrian thinkers, economics is simply the study of human action.

By clearly understanding human action, we can make sense of past financial and economic trends and get a better view of what is likely ahead. The Austrian view of the business cycle (the ups and downs of the economy) is clear and understandable. Sadly, few governments have used it to make important decisions. The results are witnessed every night on the news. But those seeking financial fitness can learn a lot from the Austrian business cycle.

The Business Cycle

The name "Austrian school" came as the result of several economists (most notably Hayek and von Mises) fleeing Austria to get away from the spread of Nazi power before World War II, during the same period as the classic movie *The Sound of Music*. This group of thinkers openly disagreed with Nazi views and was also loudly against the rising communist philosophies. Most of these economists came to the United States, and their writings on economics were infused both with the wisdom of their ideas on freedom and their personal experiences watching their nation lose its liberty.

In the Austrian view, two things cause recessions, depressions, and other downturns of the economy: 1) too much bank credit (and the debt that follows) and 2) central bank interference in economies. The problem is that these two things keep interest rates too low for too long.

When credit is too easy and interest rates are too low, the result is widespread use of debt, speculation, and the creation of economic bubbles and low savings. In short, when central banks keep credit rates lower than the free market would normally bear, a lot of people, businesses, and governments stop saving, spend what savings they did have, and then use debt to spend even more.

At the same time, there is less investment because the cost of loans is so artificially low. Businesses just use credit instead of seeking real investors (who are often wise guides and mentors). These problems usually lead to clusters of business errors in a short period of time because business managers are distracted or misled by the skewed financial numbers that accompany artificially low credit rates.

When the environment of high debt, high spending, low savings, low investment, and poor business choices gets bad enough; the market reacts and a recession occurs. Bubbles are burst, meaning that sectors of the economy with too much debt (and not enough savings) are hit especially hard.

Often a number of business errors by huge companies happen within a few months, and the bursting of more than one bubble quickly follows. This causes an economic crash.

Some crashes are small, while others are much bigger, depending on the levels of debt, spending, savings, and business error. Bad government policies can make crashes much worse. Some crashes can reach the point of depression, with 25% or higher unemployment, very little production, and other major economic problems.

Solutions That Work

The solution to economic crashes, according to the Austrian economists, is the same as the way to avoid them. First, if a nation uses the gold standard, there is really no need for a central bank in the first place. With a gold standard, banks will only be able to loan out what they have in gold reserves, so there won't be too much credit (or debt), and the whole system will remain sound.

If a nation has a gold standard but allows banks to lend more than they have in reserve, the government should regulate banks to keep the amount they lend beyond their reserves as low as possible.

Second, for the most part, governments should not intervene in the economy, but leave things to the free market. Governments should protect against major crime, fraud, and breaking of contracts, but let freedom work beyond these few cases.

Third, letting the interest rates be determined by the free market keeps bubbles from being created. Most people think low interest rates are a good thing because most people borrow a lot and save very little. If you have money in savings, however, you want interest rates to be higher because you will earn more interest. In other words, low interest rates encourage debt and overspending (by governments, businesses, and individuals), while interest rates set by the free market incentivize savings and sound investments.

The Role of Entrepreneurs

Fourth, entrepreneurs are the best people to determine which investments are sound, since they bear the risk of failure. If their investments do not succeed, the government and the people don't have to pay the burden of their losses (in a true free-market system). And if their investments are profitable, many people will benefit from the jobs they provide, the money they spend and invest from their profits (which will support more jobs and increase the profits of other businesses), and the savings they put in banks and other places.

In free economies, the things that receive the highest rewards are those that require the most risk. Thus entrepreneurs are very important contributors to society's prosperity and progress. If entrepreneurs are given the freedom to act, they will bring more affluence to the nations where they work. And with many entrepreneurs in action, those who do fail will not widely hurt the whole nation.

If entrepreneurs are not treated well in a nation, they go elsewhere and take jobs and capital with them. They take much of the nation's creativity and enterprising spirit with them as well. This always leads to decline in the nation they leave.

> If entrepreneurs are given the freedom to act, they will bring more affluence to the nations where they work.

By the way, treating entrepreneurs badly means allowing government policies of high taxes, high levels of regulation, little economic freedom, high government debt, lots of government competition in the market, or a government that is big and growing.

Free Enterprise Works, If People Let It

In short, a good economy exists when there is a good currency (gold or gold-backed) and very little government intervention in the economy, except to maintain the rules of free enterprise for everyone.

When these two things are clear and followed, free enterprise naturally encourages high savings, low debt, frugal spending, and wise investment in solid business enterprises. This maintains a more stable economy with few bubbles, crashes, or major downturns and much less violent cycles.

Some ups and downs will always occur, given the reality of wars, earthquakes and other natural disasters, and changes in the size and spending habits of generations. But in the current system in most modern nations, governments and central banks create many recessions, bubbles, and economic problems through intervention in the economy, artificially low interest rates, bad policies, printing fiat currency, and government overspending, overtaxing, over-regulating, and borrowing.

Sadly, most modern nations are addicted to high debt, low savings, high spending, and fiat currency. This applies to their governments and also to most of their citizens.

Frogs and Camels

How did we reach the point where most governments around the world are using a bad system? Many free societies started out with good systems, but slowly moved away from their strong free-enterprise roots. As we noted earlier, the ruling classes of all nations always try to turn their society into a command economy.

Interestingly, this seldom happens openly or quickly. Government "creep" toward aristocracy, socialism, and other brands of "rule by the few" is usually accomplished behind the scenes—so the middle class doesn't realize what is happing in time to vote against it. Worse, many in the middle class get duped into "worshipping" their government and enthusiastically help bind the chains that eliminate their freedom.

An old proverb teaches that the way to shift a nation from free enterprise to socialism is like boiling a frog. If you drop a frog into boiling water, it will immediately jump out. But if you put it in water at room temperature and then slowly turn up the heat, it will feel warm and comfortable until it is too late.

Chris shared a similar example in our book *LIFE*:

Traveling in caravans across the sub-Saharan deserts for centuries, traders would tie up their camels a distance far enough from their tent to prevent the camels from trying to get in. Nobody, no matter how dependent upon his camel for survival and transportation, would choose to lodge alongside his camel inside the warmth and comfort of his own tent. [Camels are notoriously dirty and covered with fleas, so people want them far away from their beds.]

The camels, however, resisted this fact. No matter how unwanted they were within the confines of their owner's tent, they still desired to partake in a little of that luxury themselves. They would start their attempt by pushing only their nose under the tent flap. If this went successfully unnoticed, they would slide the full length of their head in. Gradually, little by little, they would stick their whole neck inside, and finally their whole body.

Suddenly, the whole animal would be entirely inside the tent enjoying the shelter from the elements, crowding out the tent's rightful owner.

Government can…act in the same way. "It's just a temporary expedient until the crisis is abated," they say, sliding their nose under the flap. "Just a little while longer and we'll have this problem licked," they say, sliding in their entire neck and head. And on it goes. As President Reagan said, "There is nothing quite so permanent as a temporary government program."

The strangest fact, however, is that so many people seem intent on actually *helping* the camel sneak into the tent! But a little thought is all that's required to explain this strange situation: they don't want a camel in their *own* tent; they only want to help one get into *yours*![24]

Financial fitness includes becoming a student of your nation's history and current events. Specifically, study where your nation is on its slide toward a command economy. Pay special attention to the following: 1) historical and current changes in how your national government works, 2) the adoption of a national bank, 3) historical and current court cases that significantly alter how the nation operates, and 4) all major treaties with other nations and international organizations. These are the four biggest ways that free enterprise is lost.

In fact, the history of national banks (which intervene in interest rates and often print and issue fiat currency for the government) is essential knowledge for the financially fit.

Those who blithely ignore what is happening in the world, who figuratively stick their head in the sand and let their governments, elite classes, and central banks slowly sneak into their tent, probably deserve the flea bites they will get when the camels have moved in![25]

Include a study of history, freedom, and current events in your long-term economic plan because these things have direct impact on your finances. In the next chapter, we will discuss some specific ways to do this.

TWENTY-SIX

Prepare for the Future

When it comes to the future, there are three kinds of people: those who let it happen, those who make it happen, and those who wonder what happened.
—JOHN M. RICHARDSON

When it comes to the future, it is important to be one of the people who help make it happen. To be financially fit, it is vital to study your national economy and understand what is actually going on because the wealth you are building must fit into a larger economy. Most people do not realize this, and that is one of the reasons most people are financially flabby.

A good place to start is to analyze the economy of your nation and consider how prepared it is for small, medium, or major economic challenges in the years ahead. An excellent way to do this is to consider how your nation is applying the key principles of financial fitness.

As the economist Henry Hazlitt taught, the core principles of personal finance are directly applicable to big institutions and governments as well.

> **The core principles of personal finance are directly applicable to big institutions and governments as well.**

Rate Your Nation

To see how well your nation is doing, simply turn some of the basic things we have talked about regarding personal finance into questions about your country's economy. For example:

1. Is your nation a saver nation or a debtor nation? For example, is your government in major debt, or does it have a large surplus? Does it have *any* surplus? Does it have a deficit or a surplus this year? What about the individual savings of the citizens?

    If your nation is strong in these areas, it is prepared to weather the normal economic shocks that come along. If not, depending on how bad these things are, it may be headed for a medium or massive economic downturn.

    For example, while the U.S. national household savings rate was above 13% in 1960, in recent years, it has gone below 1%—the lowest since World War II.[26] In comparison, note the following national household savings rates:

    - Austria: 9.8%
    - Canada: 1.1%
    - France: 12.3%
    - Germany: 10.6%
    - Italy: 6.8%
    - Spain: 10.9%
    - United Kingdom: 2.5%[27]

    Many Asian nations are doing even better. For example, while statistics from China are sometimes unreliable, nearly all Western experts put China's annual savings rate above 25%.[28] One report listed the combined savings rate of China and India at 35%,[29] while many reports from these nations put the amount closer to 50%. But even at 25%, China's savings is way ahead of the United States and Canada.

In Singapore, over 17% of all households have over $1 million of wealth, compared to 4.3% in the United States.[30] The U.S. deficit is legendary, and the national debt is over $16 trillion and quickly rising. It is over $53 trillion if you include everything that is owed and promised.

What does your nation have, in cash and metal currency, in its long-term savings? Consider both government and private savings. When difficult economic times come, nations with long-term savings do much better than those with little or no savings.

We are not suggesting that big crashes are just ahead. Rather, we note that the cycles of history are up at times and down at others. Challenging times do come to every economy, just as times of peace and prosperity also come.

The rule is this: Nations that are economically strong and well-prepared for major economic downturns are less likely to have them; in contrast, nations with weak economies that are ill-prepared for major problems tend to have serious crashes and downturns.

> **Most successful people—and nations—follow a similar pattern.**

If your nation is prepared, there is less reason for concern. If your nation is unprepared, economic problems are highly likely. To be financially fit, it is important to keep an eye on these things.

2. How widespread and effective is the financial and leadership education in your nation? How many people in your country consistently live the principles of financial fitness?

    If most of the nation is financially unfit, it is likely that the nation is also out of financial shape and financial problems are more likely. Also, such a nation will not do well in times of economic downturn, so prepare your own finances accordingly.

3. What percentage of your nation are business owners versus employees? This impacts the direction and momentum of your national economy. Nations with large numbers of producers weather economic recession much better than those where the overwhelming percentage of workers are dependent on jobs and their next paycheck.

4. How much debt do your government and the private citizens have? Is the overarching culture one that avoids debt or encourages it? Debt is a serious problem that causes financial downturns, and when economic hard times occur, nations in deep debt have a hard time getting the economy back on track.

5. How much do your nation and its people have set aside for emergencies? Those with more reserves will do better in the years immediately ahead than those who are unprepared.

6. How many people in your nation live off passive income? Is the central fiscal focus of your government to have stable (gold or gold-backed) money, low taxes, and minimal regulations in order to encourage free

enterprise? If not, economic downturn will likely hit your nation, and it will probably hit especially hard.

7. How prepared are most of the people in your community and nation for a prolonged recession or depression? How long could most of them maintain their current lifestyles without more active income?

If your nation is prepared, it can more effectively weather the challenges of recession or even depression, and it is less likely to go through these things. If not, your personal and business preparation is essential. Of course, wise preparation is important even if your nation is doing well.

What Is Your Nation's Momentum?

Based on the answers to these questions, does it appear that your nation is headed for major economic problems, and if so, how likely is it that most people will survive and even flourish during down times?

The sad truth is that many nations in the world today are on the verge of serious financial challenges—or already facing them. This is true of the so-called "advanced" economies in Europe and North America, and also of some of the "Westernized-style" economies in Asia like Japan and South Korea. In contrast, a few nations, including several leading countries like China, India, and Brazil, are in much better economic shape.

As we said, the principles of financial freedom apply to individuals, families, and businesses, and they also apply to cities, states/provinces, and whole nations. If your nation is in the danger zone, like the United States and Canada, prepare yourself for economic downturns that will almost surely come.

In our view, the way to prepare is found in the principles of financial fitness covered in this book. If you live them, you will be prepared to weather the storm and even flourish if serious economic problems arise.

STUDY THE STRENGTHS AND/OR WEAKNESSES OF YOUR NATION AND ECONOMY (AND OTHERS WHERE YOU DO BUSINESS) AND WISELY CONSIDER AND PREPARE FOR POTENTIAL ECONOMIC DOWNTURNS.

If you live in a nation that is strong in these seven areas, applying the principles of financial fitness will help lead you to financial strength and prosperity. If your nation is weak in these things, living these principles will likely be absolutely necessary for you to survive financially in the years ahead.

Prosperity and wealth can still be built in such nations, but only by closely and consistently living the laws of financial fitness.

Get Connected

Another important preparation for the future is to be actively involved in your community and get connected with local leaders and groups who will take the lead in times of difficulty. Sometimes people get so focused on work and family that they don't get involved in a broader way. This is often shortsighted and foolish.

> Financial fitness means living the kind of life that brings economic success; it is not a "get-rich-quick" scheme, but a long-term focus on effective financial principles.

In the book *Rich Like Them: My Door-to-Door Search for the Secrets of Wealth in America's Richest Neighborhoods*, researcher Ryan

D'Agostino outlined several key guidelines to attaining success and wealth. These include:

- Open your eyes and notice things most people don't see.
- Take calculated risks.
- Don't deviate from your path.
- Ignore the naysayers and trust yourself.
- Obsess over the job you love.
- Connect with others.[31]

All of these are good advice, and the last point (connect with others) is very important in preparing for national or regional economic challenges. Those who do not frequently interact with people beyond their normal circles have a harder time building real financial success over time. Beyond this, during times of difficulty, many good people "wake up" and get serious about doing the right things.

If you are already connected and involved before this happens, you will have the opportunity to serve, lead, and help people when they are most invested in positive change and progress.

Do It!

Apply the principles from the last two chapters to your real life, and capture your new plans to implement these things in writing. Get serious about studying economic principles and ideas. For example, consider reading the following books on free enterprise (in the suggested order):

1. *LeaderShift* by Orrin Woodward and Oliver DeMille
2. *Economics in One Lesson* by Henry Hazlitt
3. *The Law* by Frederic Bastiat
4. *And Justice for All* by Orrin Woodward

5. *Basic Economics* by Thomas Sowell
6. *How an Economy Grows and Why It Crashes* by Peter D. Schiff
7. *Launching a Leadership Revolution* by Chris Brady and Orrin Woodward
8. *Man, Economy and State* by Murray Rothbard
9. *The Constitution of Liberty* by Friedrich Hayek
10. *Human Action* by Ludwig von Mises

Studying the great principles of economics is very important for those who want to be financially fit. What happens in society and the nations of the world has a major influence on good economic choices. Knowing the playing field is vital for financial health. Make this study a part of your long-term investment in yourself.

Summary of Part IV—Playing Field

- The principles covered in this section include:

  - PRINCIPLE 42: Studying and understanding free enterprise is an essential part of financial fitness.
  - PRINCIPLE 43: Financially fit people who want to maintain an environment that encourages opportunity and prosperity pay attention to the principles of freedom and the ongoing actions of government.
  - PRINCIPLE 44: In addition to cash savings, save some of your money in something other than fiat currency.
  - PRINCIPLE 45: Study up on investments in metal, and any other investment, before you buy. Do your homework. Take your time.
  - PRINCIPLE 46: Invest even more in yourself by learning to be the kind of person who consistently engages in an enterprising, creative, enthusiastic type of life. Fill your days with enterprise, action, and doing things that matter. And teach your children and the people you work with to do the same. Become the kind of person and leader who consistently works on your current enterprise.
  - PRINCIPLE 47: Study the strengths and/or weaknesses of your nation and economy (and others where you do business) and wisely consider and prepare for potential economic downturns.

- Get serious about studying finances, freedom, and economics.

Conclusion

Supporting Free Enterprise takes character, because it gives power to the consumers, not to the State or Big Business. Any alternative economic system denies the consumers' rights, leaving someone else as the final arbiter of the customers' wishes, making a mockery of freedom.
—Chris Brady and Orrin Woodward

Henry David Thorough famously quipped, "Most men live lives of quiet desperation." This is sadly true. The other alternative is to live the life you were born to live by achieving the mission God gave you!

You have a purpose in life, and living it is the great key to success and happiness.

Unfortunately, most people have been taught a very bad lesson, and they apply it to most areas of their lives, including finances. This negative lesson is that life is hard and that when things get difficult, the best response is to mope, feel sorry for your challenges, blame others or circumstances, and basically retreat into your shell. This is exactly the opposite of what is needed.

When life gives you challenges, respond by taking action. As the old saying goes, "It's time to do something, even if it's wrong." If you take action, you can adjust and improve. But if you don't take action, you are not going to get anywhere.

It's Simple

The truth is success is simpler than many people realize. There are principles of success in any endeavor, and when you apply correct principles, the result is that problems eventually turn around and success comes. If you are out of shape, for example, exercising and eating right will nearly always fix the problem. It's simple, but it is not always easy. In fact, success is usually very challenging—because doing great things takes great effort.

Likewise, if you want to get financially fit, follow the principles covered in this book. This is simple. And it will work. It has worked for thousands of people before you, and it will work for you.

This is worth repeating: You *can* be financially fit. The principles covered in this book work, and as soon as you begin applying some of them, you will be on the path to financial health. As we wrote in our book *LIFE*:

> Action is the key. Character is exhibited by the action of the individual in the face of paralyzing pressure. When the average person would curl up like a bug, the champion comes out swinging.
>
> Never underestimate the power of massive action to initiate a whole train of events that can pull you out of your problem. Its cumulative impact is often hard to believe. Progress stacks upon progress, challenges recede, breaks seem to happen in an increasingly positive direction, and the sky seems to clear.[32]

We believe the time has arrived for you to take massive action to become financially fit. Start with Principle 1. Reread it. Think about it. Then do it. *Just do it.*

Then do the same with Principle 2. And keep going all the way through this book. When you are living all forty-seven principles, or even just giving them your genuine best try, you are going to see amazing progress. The old question, "How do you eat an elephant?" applies here. As you know, the answer is, "One bite at a time."

Take your first bite now. Do the first seven principles in this book, the basics outlined in Part I. They're only seven "bites," but doing them will literally change your life. Do not wait. If you have not done the first seven principles yet, do them today—right now. Stay up late. Do not put this book down until you have made a real plan to implement these principles.

A Day You Will Remember

If you do this, you are going to look back on this day as a turning point in your life. You will remember this as the time you started getting financially fit—for real. These principles work. We have used them and watched them work in our own lives, and in the lives of literally thousands of others.

The first step is to pay yourself first from now on, starting today, and never skipping this vital action for the rest of your life.

The second step is to write out your life dream. This matters because without a clear dream, your efforts will mostly go to waste. You probably work hard in life. Most people do. But as Orrin says, "Working hard without a dream is like rowing a boat in the middle of the ocean without knowing the way to shore."[33] Know your dream, and your hard work will have a direction.

If you do this, you are going to look back on this day as a turning point in your life.

The truth is that most people who work hard in life still are not financially fit. Real fitness takes more than effort; it requires an accurate understanding of the financial principles outlined here. And it only comes if you apply the principles.

The good news is that when you know these forty-seven principles of financial fitness and apply them, your hard work will lead to your dreams. Again, we have seen this happen for thousands of people. We wrote this book because we want to see it happen for you, too.

The Saddest Choice

Not living your dreams really is a life of quiet desperation. As Chris says, "Not all of us die in the end. Some of us die in the middle." Do not be one of those people. Don't be normal. Don't settle for anything less than your best. Living the laws of financial success is not hard. It just takes focus.

It is amazing how simple it really is to get financially fit, and yet so many people do not bother to do it. They either don't know what to do, or they think the principles of financial fitness are too difficult or don't apply to them.

This reminds us of the story about a woman who wanted to go on a luxury cruise. She pinched pennies and saved for years, foregoing many small pleasures in order to put away cash for her dream cruise. She read about different cruises, imagining the day she would stand on the top deck and watch the gorgeous Mediterranean Sea and the shorelines of Greece, France, Spain, and Italy.

She saved and saved, and finally the big day came. Enthusiastically, she got on the boat, took part in the activities, and enjoyed the sun and the beautiful scenes for a week. To save money on her limited budget, she skipped the main meals and bought small snacks in the gift shop. She was a bit hungry most of the week, but she loved the whole experience.

On the last day, a new friend from the cruise invited her to dinner. She replied that she could not really afford it. The friend was surprised and asked her, "Don't you know that the meals are all included in the price of your ticket?"

Too many people are like this woman as they go through life. There are so many experiences, blessings, and opportunities that are included in the price of admission to this life, yet they miss out on them simply because they do not understand the big picture.

This is incredibly sad. The principles are clear and proven. All that is required is action, but so many people just don't ever get around to applying the principles of success. As Orrin puts it, "Most are playing it safe in life, even though none of us is getting out alive."

> **It is amazing how simple it really is to get financially fit, and yet so many people do not bother to do it. Be different!**

Enjoy the Journey!

But here is the good news. You never have to be financially flabby again. You know the principles. You know they work. Now take action. Apply them. Start with Principle 1, then Principle 2, then Principle 3, and so on. Do not let anything stand in the way of living your dreams, especially something as simple as not applying these basic principles. Create an avalanche of financial health by living these principles one snowflake at a time.

And have fun with it. Don't take life too seriously. Remember the following definition:

Shin: A device for finding furniture in the dark.

If you are not laughing at that, read it again. Turn up both corners of your mouth and see how that feels. It's really pretty cool. In English, it's known as a "smile."

Seriously, people tend to take things way too seriously. So many people forget that life is supposed to be a lot of fun. Do yourself a favor and allow a lot more humor into your life! Laugh a lot. Smile most of the time. As you apply the principles of financial fitness, you will naturally start experiencing more humor, laughter, and fun in your life. The principles are that powerful.

So relax. When you are applying the principles of success, you can just let go and enjoy life. Let the principles do the heavy lifting for you. That is what principles are for, after all. They let you put so many things on autopilot, so you can focus on the things that matter most.

You can scrimp and eat small snacks and skip the meals that are already paid for with your ticket to the cruise called life, or you can apply the principles of financial fitness and enjoy the great results they will bring you. The choice is clear: You can live a life of quiet desperation, or you can live a life of experiencing your dreams.

Going Bowling

Most people miss out because they don't think it could really be this simple. They are like beginning bowlers who keep their eyes on the pins and keep rolling gutter balls. Then someone teaches them to keep their eyes on the lines painted near the front of the lane, and they suddenly start hitting strikes, or at least a lot of pins.

The principles of financial fitness are like the lines in bowling lanes, and by focusing on them consistently, you will hit a lot more of your dreams. Without the principles, you are going to face a life of continual financial gutter balls.

A Call to Greatness

So start today. Use these principles. We believe they will change your life. You have too much greatness ahead of you to wait any longer. It is time to get financially fit. You know what to do. Now is the right time to begin.

And don't do it just for you. The world needs you to be financially fit. It needs you to live your dreams, dreams that can only happen if you have the resources and time to do them. Your example of financial fitness can help others rise to their potential as well. Indeed, we need a revolution of financial fitness right now in today's world.

Where are the leaders, entrepreneurs, and dreamers who will step up to the plate and swing for the fences?[34] We need to fix families, faith, freedom, finances, and other things in the world. And it is only going to happen if more people stop living under the slavery of financial problems.

The time has come to send out a call to all who care about the future. It's time to take a stand. If we wait much longer, it will be too late for most people.

The best news is that this is really a very simple process. You have learned the principles of financial fitness. Now live them. Apply them today and every day from now on. We believe this one change will make all the difference—in your life and the lives of everyone you influence in the years ahead.

It's time to take action. It's time to change your life. It's time to get financially fit.

Throughout this book, each chapter has taught the principles of financial fitness and then ended with a call to implement what you have learned with real-life change by taking action. Learning isn't actually learning unless you apply it.

> Are you one of the leaders, entrepreneurs, and dreamers who will step up to the plate and swing for the fences? The world needs you to be financially fit. It's time to take a stand!

Now, as you finish this book, you are in a unique position. You know something that only a few people in the world know. You know the principles of financial fitness. You know what to do to become financially healthy. You know how to set the example for others so they can do the same. You know what the people around you need to do to get their financial lives in order. And you know what your nation needs to do as well.

That is a lot to know because knowledge really is power. But it only makes a positive difference in the world if you put it into practice. You have taken the first step by reading this book, and that is good. But the next step is ahead, and you know you are going to take it. You know what you are going to do next.

There are forty-seven fundamentals of financial fitness, and you are going to live them.

You are going to live them for the rest of your life.

Starting *now*.

The 47 Principles of Financial Fitness

Basics

PRINCIPLE 1: It's not what you make but what you keep that determines financial success. Pay yourself first and save what you pay yourself.

PRINCIPLE 2: Money is a gift. It has a specific use. This means that you have a stewardship. You are to use your money for something that matters, for your family and beyond.

PRINCIPLE 3: Live within your means. Always. No exceptions. Period. Follow a good budget. Give each spouse a small allowance so you have a little discretionary money each month, and don't nitpick each other on the little things.

PRINCIPLE 4: Stop getting financial advice from broke people; get it only from those whose finances you want to emulate.

PRINCIPLE 5: Consistently budget and save for unexpected expenses.

PRINCIPLE 6: Pay 10% of your income to tithing. Give even if you are really broke. Giving puts you in a mindset of abundance and puts any financial worries in their proper perspective, so it should not be limited to just tithing. The Bible categorizes giving as: 1) tithes and 2) offerings.

PRINCIPLE 7: Using your time, money, and talents to genuinely help others naturally increases your happiness. Seeking money for money's sake may or may not influence your happiness, but seeking money in order to fulfill your stewardship and serve and bless others automatically increases it.

Offense

PRINCIPLE 8: People with the right moneyview discipline themselves to live the principles of financial fitness, make financial decisions based on a long-term vision, adopt the habit of delayed gratification, and use the compounding nature of money to constructively achieve their dreams.

PRINCIPLE 9: Financially fit people are avid readers and consistently invest in themselves by increasing their financial and leadership education, skills, experience, knowledge, and ability.

PRINCIPLE 10: Financially fit people excel at the work and projects they are doing now, and at the same time, they invest in themselves in order to achieve their long-term vision.

PRINCIPLE 11: Never sacrifice principles for money or possessions. Be honest. Keep your integrity. Keep your priorities in the right order.

PRINCIPLE 12: Do the work to gain mastery in what you do (usually about 10,000 hours).

PRINCIPLE 13: Financially fit people don't ask "Can we afford it?" as much as they ask "Do we *really* want this? Will it help our purpose and dream? *How* will it help our purpose and dream? In what ways might it be a distraction? Will it cost more money to take care of it or keep it (through things like insurance or annual fees)? Would saving or investing the same amount be a bigger help to our purpose and vision? Is *now* the best time for this purchase, or would it be less expensive or just better for our family or business at a later date?" They cultivate a habit of saying "No" to purchases even when they can easily afford them and of putting much of their money into savings or investments instead.

PRINCIPLE 14: Financially fit people analyze their habits—in life as well as finances—and work to break bad habits and cultivate good ones. They think about and choose the habits they want and need to achieve their life dreams.

PRINCIPLE 15: Own a business, even if you start out working on it part-time. You can apply all the other principles in this book and obtain wealth over time, but those who apply them in their own businesses can become wealthy much more quickly.

PRINCIPLE 16: Increase your passive income to the point that 1) most of your income is passive and 2) you can live off your passive income.

PRINCIPLE 17: Retirement should not be an issue of age but rather a function of having enough passive income to live on for life. Retirement means retiring from things that are not part of your purpose so you can focus your productive work on your life mission.

PRINCIPLE 18: To really attain financial success, focus on these things: 1) Truly excel in your current job and projects and simultaneously start a business, 2) Put in the 10,000 or so hours needed to gain mastery over your business while still excelling at your current job, 3) Make a plan to become financially free by reaching a point where the passive income from your business more than covers your family's needs, and 4) Once you are financially free, put your full-time focus on building your business to the point that it funds your life purpose. Each of these requires deep focus, one at a time. Once you have accomplished one of them, go to the next and give it the same level of focus.

PRINCIPLE 19: Get good mentors and really listen to them.

PRINCIPLE 20: Use your money productively—by putting it where it will bring you back more than you put in—rather than nonproductively. The best investment is in yourself and your own business. Wisely and appropriately use some of your savings to increase your business assets and returns.

PRINCIPLE 21: Put some money into preparing for a worst-case scenario. Don't be fanatical about this, but don't ignore it either.

PRINCIPLE 22: Build up a regular targeted savings fund for things you want to buy later. Consistently fund this account and buy consumer items with cash (not financing).

PRINCIPLE 23: Only invest money you can afford to lose entirely in speculations outside your area(s) of mastery. Only invest a little, if any, in such ventures.

PRINCIPLE 24: Do not ever use your savings to speculate.

Defense

PRINCIPLE 25: Get rid of debt.

PRINCIPLE 26: If you aren't financially sound, don't get caught in the trap of using "business debt."

PRINCIPLE 27: Do not use credit cards to build your credit because this almost always leads people to more debt.

PRINCIPLE 28: Never use title pawning, "ninety-days-same-as-cash" loans, payday loans, rent-to-own plans, layaway debt, or similar schemes.

PRINCIPLE 29: See your car(s) as transportation, not status symbols. Save up and always pay cash for them.

PRINCIPLE 30: Debit cards are better than credit cards for many people, and cash is even better.

PRINCIPLE 31: Teach your children and youth the principles of financial fitness. Set the example for them. Mentoring them will help you as well as them.

PRINCIPLE 32: If you are not wealthy, do not get sucked in to using second mortgages.

PRINCIPLE 33: Use the roll-down method to pay off all credit card debts and then apply it to all other debts.

PRINCIPLE 34: Learn to be skeptical of advertising, media, and marketing.

PRINCIPLE 35: Accumulate slowly; build your inventory of resources and wisdom, not stuff.

PRINCIPLE 36: Get right with God, apply true principles in all areas of life including finances, pursue your stewardship, serve others—and leave impressing others in God's hands.

PRINCIPLE 37: Do not use consumer debt. Wise financing for business investment may be okay at times, but consumer debt is like a cancer. Cut it out!

PRINCIPLE 38: Make memories part of your lifestyle, budget, and life plan. Start simple and add big memories, too.

PRINCIPLE 39: Be very, very careful as you make decisions about the danger zones: taxes, home ownership, divorce, credit cards, lawsuits, insurance, seeking status, college, addictions, and investments. Get good advice from your financial mentors, and study things in detail before taking action.

PRINCIPLE 40: If you buy a home, follow the 2X Rule. For example, if your income is $50,000 per year, do not buy a home that costs more than $100,000. If you want a bigger home, earn more money.

PRINCIPLE 41: If you are not financially fit and you have a bunch of "toys," it means that you do not really deserve them and you are using your savings or debt on the wrong things. If your debts are all paid off, you are following the savings guidelines listed in earlier principles, and you have the cash, you can buy a few "toys" and still be financially fit.

Playing Field

PRINCIPLE 42: Studying and understanding free enterprise is an essential part of financial fitness.

PRINCIPLE 43: Financially fit people who want to maintain an environment that encourages opportunity and prosperity pay attention to the principles of freedom and the ongoing actions of government.

271

PRINCIPLE 44: In addition to cash savings, save some of your money in something other than fiat currency.

PRINCIPLE 45: Study up on investments in metal, and any other investment, before you buy. Do your homework. Take your time.

PRINCIPLE 46: Invest even more in yourself by learning to be the kind of person who consistently engages in an enterprising, creative, enthusiastic type of life. Fill your days with enterprise, action, and doing things that matter. And teach your children and the people you work with to do the same. Become the kind of person and leader who consistently works on your current enterprise.

PRINCIPLE 47: Study the strengths and/or weaknesses of your nation and economy (and others where you do business) and wisely consider and prepare for potential economic downturns.

Glossary

24 Hour Rule: The principle that if you see an excellent deal, or any other deal for that matter, you should wait at least twenty-four hours before you buy. Think about the purchase and determine whether it will be an investment or just money used and gone.

2X Rule: The principle that you should not buy a home that costs more than twice what you make annually.

Active vs. Passive Income: Active income is earned as a result of work you do, so it requires your active participation to get it; passive income keeps paying you even if you stop working.

Assets vs. Liabilities: An asset is something you own that brings you additional money while a liability is something you own that costs you additional money.

Barter Economy: An economic system with no currency, where people trade actual products or services in order to meet their needs. Such economies always remain primitive.

Budget: A plan of how to spend your income. A good budget accurately outlines income and keeps expenditures lower than income.

Build Your Pipeline: A phrase used to communicate the effectiveness of building your business or other income streams to consistently increase your passive income. Those without a pipeline frequently struggle to create lasting prosperity.

Command Economy: An economic system where one person, or a small group of elites, makes many of the important decisions for everyone.

Commodity vs. Fiat Money: Commodity money has value for its own sake, such as eggs or cattle or gold, while fiat money only has value because a government says so. Through history, the government backing of fiat money has proven unstable and risky.

Compound Interest: Interest paid on both the principal and the accrued interest. You are charged interest on something you financed, and then on a later day, you are also charged interest on the earlier interest. People who pay compound interest usually end up spending much more money than their purchases are worth, while those who collect it make money faster than others.

Creditors: People or entities to which a person or business owes money.

Debt: Money a person owes to someone or some entity. Most debt should be avoided, especially consumer debt.

Delayed Gratification: The state of waiting to spend money on things until you can truly afford them.

Depreciation: The decrease in value of an asset over time. Never use credit to finance something that depreciates.

Economics: The study of human action and all its ramifications. Understanding economics is essential for financial fitness.

Emergency Fund: A fund that covers unexpected or emergency expenses when they come. Those who are financially fit consistently (and often automatically) pay some of their income to this fund with the goal of accumulating at least three to six months worth of living expenses.

Enterprise: Taking action, often with risk, in order to achieve one's goals. Nations that encourage enterprise through freedom are more prosperous than those that do not.

Entrepreneur: A person who takes the risk to build things and create increased value and profits. Societies that incentivize entrepreneurial success are more free and prosperous than others.

Financial Danger Zone: A situation that is likely to cause significant financial problems without wise planning and decision making.

Financial Fitness: The state of understanding and applying the forty-seven laws of financial success covered in this book.

Financial Matrix: The name given to the largely invisible complicated web of fractional-reserve banking, Federal Reserve banking, and other financial instrumentation that makes it difficult for average people to "make it out alive" financially.

Financial Myth: A fake principle of finance that is widely believed but ultimately false.

Free-Enterprise Economy: An economic system where the government treats everyone equally, protecting their inalienable rights and leaving everything else to the people. When the level of free enterprise decreases, the barriers to financial success always increase.

Gold Standard: A system in which the currency of a nation is made of gold (and silver for smaller amounts) or directly and easily redeemable for gold or silver. Nations that use the gold standard make prosperity more attainable for more people.

Good Currency: The traditional definition of good currency is that it has the following four characteristics: longevity, divisibility, measurability, and transportability. But this leaves many currencies that are unstable and easily tampered with by banks, governments, and others. Thus, good currency must also have the characteristics of stability and "untamperability." Only gold and silver have met all six of these criteria through human history.

Goose That Lays the Golden Eggs: Your business or career that is the source of your financial success. Taking care of the goose means taking actions to ensure that your income will continue.

Impounding: Saving money in a safe place for a worst-case scenario.

Inflation: A decrease in the value of money due to a persistent, substantial rise in the general level of prices related to an increase in the volume of money. Government printing of fiat money often causes this.

Insolvent: Not having enough money to pay one's bills and debts.

Invest in Yourself: To devote time, money, effort, etc. to things that will increase or improve your own knowledge, mastery of what you do for a living, financial and leadership education, personal abilities, business, and so on. Investing in yourself is the most important investment you can make.

Investment vs. Spending Multiplier: The principle that more spending than investment naturally leads to even more spending and decreased financial fitness while more investment than spending creates better financial fitness. (Investment occurs when money is used to purchase something that will bring more money to the investor; spending happens when money is used to purchase something that will not bring more money to the spender and may even cost the spender more money in the future.)

Life Purpose: A person's major goals, dreams, and means of service in life.

Live within Your Means: A phrase asserting that you should not spend more than you have. This is essential to financial fitness.

Macroeconomics vs. Microeconomics: Macroeconomics is the field of human action that deals with large-scale factors such as interest rates, inflation, national taxes and spending, sectors of the economy, etc., while microeconomics deals with the actions and economic choices of individuals, small groups, and individual businesses.

Make It Automatic: Arranging to have a percentage of your income automatically diverted for a specific purpose, such as directly depositing money into your savings account(s) or paying tithes and debts, before you receive payment.

Mastery: Command or grasp, as of a subject. Financially fit people gain mastery in their area of expertise, the career or business that brings them most of their income. Those who do not gain real mastery often struggle to succeed financially.

Mentor: A wise and trusted counselor or teacher/an influential senior sponsor or supporter. A good financial mentor is one who has achieved what you want to achieve and is living the kind of life you want to emulate.

Mindset of Abundance vs. Mindset of Scarcity: A general mindset of abundance is a belief that good things will come to those who learn and apply true principles, while a scarcity mindset is a belief that you can't or won't succeed regardless of what you do. Financially fit people adopt an abundant mindset and apply the principles of financial fitness.

Moneyview: A person's beliefs and perspective on money, its value and purpose in life, and how to obtain and use it.

National Momentum: The economic direction in which individuals and businesses work, which is determined by how closely a nation follows the principles of financial fitness.

Offerings: Money beyond tithing that you give to help others and support worthy causes.

Pay Yourself First: This is the first principle and one of the most important factors of financial fitness. People who consistently pay themselves first and always keep this money in savings are nearly all financially fit.

Principal and Interest: Principal is the original amount of money lent, while interest is the amount you pay to borrow the money to buy something. Sometimes the interest actually costs more than the principal. Always find out what the actual cost will be by adding the principal and all of the interest you will have to pay. In most cases, avoid paying interest.

Principle: A universal truth that, if applied correctly, always works.

Productive Use of Money: Spending money on something that will bring you back more money.

Prosperity: The state of being financially fit and seeing your finances succeed and flourish because you have learned and applied the laws of financial fitness.

Rainy-Day Fund: See "Emergency Fund."

Retirement Rule: You are ready to retire when you have enough passive income to live on for life.

Reward: A benefit you give yourself when you meet a preset financial goal.

Roll-Down Method: A technique of getting out of debt by paying off your smaller debts first and then using the payment amount from the smaller debt to help pay off the next smallest debt—and continuing this process until all of your debts are retired.

Savings: Money you put away each time you receive income and which you never spend. The level of your savings is the measure of your prosperity.

Savings Accounts: There are several kinds of savings accounts, or money kept in banks. One is the **emergency fund,** in which people put away savings (with the goal of having at least three to six months worth of living expenses) for a rainy day, including unexpected expenses such as a broken stove or burned-up car engine. A second is the **long-term savings**, where people put away money in order to build more wealth. A third is a **targeted savings fund**, where people save money for special planned purchases such as a car, a trip, college for a child, etc.

Shopaholism: The habit of spending, often using consumer debt, for things you do not really need.

Specialization: The division of labor into different areas of work and expertise. Specialization allows individuals to gain mastery over different fields and then exchange the fruits of their labor. Societies that encourage specialization are usually more prosperous than those that do not.

Spending Multiplier: This occurs when people spend so much on things they do not really need that they create a momentum to spend more and more. This is a serious financial disease that causes many financial problems.

Spontaneous Purchases: Buying things in the moment without taking the time to really consider the wisdom of the purchase. See "24 Hour Rule."

Status Trap: The allurement of looking successful and important that can cause people to spend beyond their means to keep up appearances when they are in fact financially broke.

Stewardship: The responsible overseeing and protection of your money, assets, energies, and other resources in order to truly build God's kingdom in the way you feel is best suited to your calling in life.

Stuff: Things you own that you do not need and should sell. Also, things you do not really need that you should not buy.

Tithing: Giving 10% of your income to your church or other appropriate recipient.

Transformational Reading: Applying what you read in ways that make a huge positive difference in your life.

Trying to Impress Others: Making efforts to appear to have achieved a higher status and level of success than one really has. This is one of the main reasons people are financially unfit. See "Status Trap."

Unexpected Expenses: Bills and costs that arise in surprising ways and amounts. Those who have an emergency fund are prepared for such expenses.

Wealth: The state of having a pipeline of passive income that keeps paying you more than you need for your bills, expenses, and enjoyments; the excess is often used by financially fit people to serve and improve the world in important ways.

Woodward Rule: Orrin Woodward's axiom that some realtors will try to convince you to spend more on a home than you should. See "2X Rule."

Written Financial Plan: A person's written outline of financial goals, strategies, and applications of the principles of financial success.

YOU, Inc.: A term used to convey the need for a person to view him- or herself as a business that needs to be built into a stronger and more profitable entity over time.

YOU, Inc. Investment Hierarchy: A hierarchy that prioritizes the various investment categories into levels of significance.

Notes

1. *The Matrix*, released March 31, 1999 (USA), written and directed by Andy and Lana (Larry) Wachowski (as The Wachowski Brothers).
2. Chris Brady and Orrin Woodward, *LIFE*, p. 23.
3. Chris Brady and Orrin Woodward, *Launching a Leadership Revolution*, p. 4. Emphasis added.
4. Brady and Woodward, *LIFE*, p. 23.
5. Brady and Woodward, *Launching a Leadership Revolution*, pp. 3-4.
6. Ibid., p. 4.
7. George Clason, *The Richest Man in Babylon*, p. 65.
8. Not a scientific statistic.
9. Alexandr Solzhenitsyn, "A World Split Apart."
10. See *Outliers* by Malcolm Gladwell and *Talent Is Overrated* by Geoffrey Colvin for more discussion of this theme.
11. Robert P. Miles, 2004, *Warren Buffett Wealth*, p. 70.
12. Ibid., p. 138.
13. LouAnn Loften, "Invest Like a Girl (and Warren Buffett)," *U.S. News & World Report*, Special Edition: Special Report: *Secrets of the Rich*, 2012, pp. 20-24.
14. "Discourses on Davila," John Carey, ed., *The Political Writings of John Adams*, pp. 323-325.
15. "The Truth Shall Set You Free Indeed, Part II," November 7, 2012, claude-hamilton.com.
16. Harper's Index, *Harpers*, August 2011.
17. Addison Wiggin, foreward to *Gold: The Once and Future Money* by Nathan Lewis.
18. Nathan Lewis, *Gold: The Once and Future Money*, flyleaf. Comments in brackets added.

19. See www.usgoldandsilveradvisors.com.

20. Chris Brady and Orrin Woodward, "Introduction to Economics," LIFE Leadership audio.

21. *Online Etymology Dictionary.*

22. Brady and Woodward, "Introduction to Economics."

23. See William Strauss and Neil Howe, *The Fourth Turning.*

24. Brady and Woodward, *LIFE,* p. 133.

25. Ibid., p. 133-134.

26. Laurence Kotlikoff, "It's the National Savings Rate, Stupid," August 6, 2010, www.kotlikoff.net.

27. OECD Economic Outlook 83 database, 2009 rates.

28. See Sheldon Garon, "Why the Chinese Save," *Foreign Policy,* January 19, 2012.

29. www.usgoldandsilveradvisors.com.

30. See Emily Jane Fox, "Number of Millionaires See a Decline in Wealth," *CNN Money,* June 4, 2012.

31. See Ryan D'Agostino, "What the Wealthy Know," *U.S. News & World Report*, Special Edition: Special Report: *Secrets of the Rich,* 2012, pp. 8-11.

32. Brady and Woodward, *LIFE,* p. 74.

33. Ibid., p. 139.

34. Ibid., p. 188.

ACKNOWLEDGMENTS

No book is the work of a single creative mind. There are always collaborations, contributions, and inputs from many sources. This book, even more than usual, is the product of the collective input of many passionate participants. Oliver DeMille's contribution is greatly appreciated. Thanks are also due to Laurie Woodward, Terri Brady, Tim and Amy Marks, Claude and Lana Hamilton, Bill Lewis, Dan and Lisa Hawkins, George and Jill Guzzardo, and Wayne and Raylene MacNamara. Thanks also go out to all the individuals who utilized our financial education and allowed us to quote them and tell their stories in the manuscript. Randy Robson did a wonderful job with research and creative direction, as well as much of the heavy lifting on the accompanying workbook. Deborah Brady, Michelle Turner, and Wendy Branson did a tremendous job on overall editing and professionalization of the book, saving us from ourselves once again. Bill Rousseau, as usual, kept the whole project on track against the ticking clock. Norm Williams worked his usual magic in developing the cover art and design. Ryan Renz, Emily O'Boyle, Andy Garcia, Jordan Woodward, and Chris Janes helped conceive, produce, and edit the accompanying video trailers and audio recordings. William Sankbeil and his staff provided excellent legal guidance. And as usual, Rob Hallstrand did an exceptional job coordinating all of the various efforts at Obstaclés Press. To all of you, may your praises be sung from the heights!

FINANCIAL FITNESS PROGRAM

Get Out of Debt and Stay Out of Debt!

FREE PERSONAL WEBSITE

SIGN UP AND TAKE ADVANTAGE OF THESE FREE FEATURES:

- Personal website
- Take your custom assessment test
- Build your own profile
- Share milestones and successes with partners and friends
- Post videos and photos
- Receive daily info "nuggets"

FINANCIAL FITNESS BASIC PROGRAM

The first program to teach all three aspects of personal finance: defense, offense, and playing field. Learn the simple, easy-to-apply principles that can help you shore up your resources, get out of debt, and build stability for a more secure future. It's all here, including a comprehensive book, companion workbook, and 8 audios that amplify the teachings from the books.

Also available DIGITALLY!

FINANCIAL FITNESS MASTER CLASS

Buy it once and use it forever! Designed to provide a continual follow-up to the principles learned in the Basic Program, this ongoing educational support offers over 6 hours of video and over 14 hours of audio instruction that walk you through the workbook, step by step. Perfect for individual or group study.
6 videos, 15 audios

FINANCIAL FITNESS TRACK AND SAVE

The Financial Fitness Program teaches you how to get out of debt, build additional streams of income, and properly take advantage of tax deductions. Now, with this subscription, we give you the tools to do so. The Tracker offers mobile expense tracking tools and budgeting software, while the Saver offers you thousands of coupons and discounts to help you save money every day.

CHRIS BRADY

New York Times bestselling author Chris Brady has sold over a million copies of his books in six different languages and is listed among the Top 100 Authors to Follow on Twitter (@RascalTweets). Some of his most popular works include *Leadership Lessons from the Age of Fighting Sail*, *PAiLS*, *A Month of Italy* (2013 Gold ADDY winner and featured in the movie *A Long Way Off*), *Rascal* (Gold Medal winner in the 2013 Living Now Evergreen Book Awards), *Launching a Leadership Revolution*, *Edge*, *Leadership and Liberty*, *Leadership: Tidbits and Treasures*, and *LIFE*.

Chris is founder, CEO, and Creative Director of LIFE Leadership and also serves as Executive Publisher of Obstaclés Press and Vice President of the All Grace Outreach charity. In 2015, he was named the #2 Humorist to Follow on Twitter, and he made the list for The Top 20 Most Followed Leadership Gurus on Twitter. He also made the Likeable Local's Top 150 Great Marketers to Follow in 2015, and he was named one of Modern Servant Leader's Top Leadership Experts to Follow in 2015. In May of 2014, Chris was ranked number 39 on *Inc.* magazine's Top 50 Leadership and Management Experts. In 2010, he received the Kettering/GMI Alumni Association Entrepreneurial Achievement Award. In addition, his blog (chrisbrady.com) has been chosen by Online Masters Degree Programs for a Masters Award in Leadership, selected as a Top Management Resource for 2012, and listed in the Top 150 Management and Leadership Blogs.

Chris earned his bachelor of science degree in mechanical engineering at Kettering University and his master of science degree in manufacturing engineering from Carnegie Mellon University as a General Motors Fellow. He conducted his master's thesis work at Toyohashi University in Japan.

Chris is an avid motorized adventurer, world traveler, private pilot, community builder, soccer fan, Christian, historian, and dad. He also has one of the world's most unique résumés, including experience with a live bug in his ear, walking through a paned glass window, chickening out from the high dive in elementary school, destroying the class ant farm in third grade, losing a spelling bee on the word *use*, jackhammering his foot, and more recently, sinking his snowmobile in a lake. Chris and his wife Terri have four children and live in North Carolina.

ORRIN WOODWARD

New York Times bestselling author of *Launching a Leadership Revolution* and *LeaderShift* Orrin Woodward has sold over a million copies of his books in six languages. His first solo book, *RESOLVED: 13 Resolutions for LIFE*, was named an All-Time Top 100 Leadership Book, and its 13 resolutions are the framework for the top-selling *Mental Fitness Challenge* personal development program. Some of his other most popular works include *The Leadership Train, And Justice for All* (which helped him become the GUINNESS WORLD RECORDS® Official Record Holder for the Largest Book Signing, with 6,786 copies of the book signed in just six hours and thirty-three minutes), the *RESOLVED Primer, Edge, Leadership and Liberty, Leadership: Tidbits and Treasures*, and *LIFE*.

Orrin is founder and Chairman of the Board of LIFE Leadership and Obstaclés Press. He also serves as President of the All Grace Outreach charity. He earned his bachelor of science degree in mechanical engineering from Kettering University (formerly GMI Engineering & Management Institute) and received business administration training from the University of Michigan.

In 2015, he was named one of the Top 20 Most Followed Leadership Gurus on Twitter, he was listed in *Inc.* magazine's Top 100 Speakers, and he was listed in Modern Servant Leader's Top Leadership Experts to Follow in 2015. In 2014, he was ranked number 20 on *Inc.* magazine's Top 50 Leadership and Management Experts. His leadership blog (orrinwoodwardblog.com) has received international acclaim as one of HR's Top 100 Blogs for Management and Leadership and as a Universities Online Top 100 Leadership Blog. Kettering/GMI University honored him as the 2010 Entrepreneur of the Year (along with Chris Brady). And as an engineer in the automotive industry, Orrin was awarded four U.S. patents and won an exclusive National Technical Benchmarking Award.

Orrin and his wife Laurie (married in 1991) have four children (Jordan, Christina, Lance, and Jeremy) and a golden retriever with a bad hip named Socrates (aka "Socks"). Orrin enjoys yachting, boating, fishing, reading, writing, traveling, playing basketball, running, and bodybuilding. He and his family follow the sun between residences in Michigan and Florida.